D0760832

DATE DUE

RIVERS
of the
WORLD

The Colorado

Titles in the Rivers of the World series include:

RIVERS
of the
WORLD

The Colorado

James Barter

LUCENT
BOOKS

THOMSON
GALE

San Diego • Detroit • New York • San Francisco • Cleveland • New Haven, Conn. • Waterville, Maine • London • Munich

On Cover: A kayaker paddles over rapids beside jagged canyon walls
on the Colorado River in Grand Canyon National Park, Arizona.

LIBRARY OF CONGRESS CATALOGING-IN-PUBLICATION DATA

Barter, James, 1946–
   The Colorado / by James Barter.
      p. cm. — (Rivers of the world)
      Summary: Describes the course of the Colorado River, its impact on the land
through which it flows and on the people living nearby, dams and canals used to har-
ness the river's water, and controversies surrounding its use.
   Includes bibliographical references and index.
   ISBN 1-59018-059-3 (lib. bdg. : alk. paper)
  1. Colorado River (Colo.-Mexico)—Juvenile literature. [1. Colorado River (Colo.-
Mexico)] I. Title. II. Series: Rivers of the World (Lucent Books)
   F788 .B28 2003
   979.1'3—dc21

2002013067

Printed in the United States of America

Contents

• • • • • • • • • • • • •

Foreword

· · · · · · · · · · · · ·

Human history and rivers are inextricably intertwined. Of all the geologic wonders of nature, none has played a more central and continuous role in the history of civilization than rivers. Fanning out across every major landmass except the Antarctic, all great rivers wove an arterial network that played a pivotal role in the inception of early civilizations and in the evolution of today's modern nation-states.

More than ten thousand years ago, when nomadic tribes first began to settle into small, stable communities, they discovered the benefits of cultivating crops and domesticating animals. These incipient civilizations developed a dependence on continuous flows of water to nourish and sustain their communities and food supplies. As small agrarian towns began to dot the Asian and African continents, the importance of rivers escalated as sources of community drinking water, as places for washing clothes, for sewage removal, for food, and as means of transportation. One by one, great riparian civilizations evolved whose collective fame is revered today, including ancient Mesopotamia, between the Tigris and Euphrates Rivers; Egypt, along the Nile; India, along the Ganges and Indus Rivers; and China, along the Yangtze. Later, for the same reasons, early civilizations in the Americas gravitated to the major rivers of the New World such as the Amazon, Mississippi, and Colorado.

For thousands of years, these rivers admirably fulfilled their role in nature's cycle of birth, death, and renewal. The waters also supported the rise of nations and their expanding populations. As hundreds and then thousands of cities sprang up along major rivers, today's modern nations emerged and discovered modern uses for the rivers. With more mouths to feed than ever before, great irrigation canals supplied by river water fanned out across the landscape, transforming parched land into mile upon mile of fertile cropland. Engineers developed the mathematics needed to throw great concrete dams across rivers to control occasional flooding and to store trillions of gallons of water to irrigate crops during the hot summer months. When the great age of electricity arrived, engineers added to the demands placed on rivers by using their cascading water to drive huge hydroelectric turbines to light and heat homes and skyscrapers in urban settings. Rivers also played a major role in the development of modern factories as sources of water for processing a variety of commercial goods and as a convenient place to discharge various types of refuse.

For a time, civilizations and rivers functioned in harmony. Such a benign relationship, however, was not destined to last. At the end of the twentieth century, scientists confirmed the opinions of environmentalists: The viability of all major rivers of the world was threatened. Urban populations could no longer drink the fetid water, masses of fish were dying from chemical toxins, and microorganisms critical to the food chain were disappearing along with the fish species at the top of the chain. The great hydroelectric dams had altered the natural flow of rivers, blocking migratory fish routes. As the twenty-first century unfolds, all who have contributed to spoiling the rivers are now in agreement that immediate steps must be taken to heal the rivers if their partnership with civilization is to continue.

Each volume in the Lucent Rivers of the World series tells the unique and fascinating story of a great river and its people. The significance of rivers to civilizations is emphasized to highlight both their historical role and present situation. Each volume illustrates the idiosyncrasies of one great river in terms of its physical attributes, the plants and animals that depend on it, its role in ancient and modern cultures, how it served the needs of the people, misuse of the river, and steps now being taken to remedy its problems.

Introduction

· · · · · · · · · · · · · · · · · · · ·

A Hardworking River

The Colorado River is the hardest-working river in the western United States. More than 35 million people in seven states and Mexico depend on the river's continuous flow for their livelihoods or well-being. Its water is put to so many uses that its glistening reddish flow, which inspired its Spanish name, rarely reaches the ocean anymore. In the arid Southwest, which has experienced the fastest population growth of any region in the United States over the past fifty years, the Colorado River is not just the most important source of open water for the thirsty millions, it is the only one capable of sustaining their water-dependent lives.

The present demands on the Colorado are indeed daunting. The river supplies water necessary for crop production, household needs, industrial use, and hydroelectric generation; it also serves as a home for a diverse collection of wildlife. To serve human demands along the river's fourteen-hundred-mile journey, its water is captured by twenty hydroelectric plants, ten additional major dams, and eighty diversion canals. Without the Colorado, major metropolitan centers such as Denver, Phoenix,

Las Vegas, San Diego, and Los Angeles would not be flourishing today.

During the ten thousand years that humans have lived near its banks, the Colorado River has successfully fulfilled these diverse demands. Within the past two decades, however, scientists and other observers have noted signs that all is no longer well along the Colorado River basin. A gauntlet of dams and canals that interrupt the free flow of water and daily divert billions of gallons from the river's natural course have taken a terrible toll on the Colorado's health. Declining water quality, water shortages, and increasing numbers of endangered species are just some of the warning signals that have alarmed the scientific and environmental communities.

The river's health is only one of two major concerns. The other involves ownership of the river's water. The Colorado flows through several states before crossing the Mexican border, and as it moves south, its volume diminishes significantly as canals direct its water away from the river toward growing cities and expanding croplands. Questions regarding who has the right to use the water,

The Hoover Dam, one of ten major dams on the Colorado River, diverts the river's water to supply many cities, including Denver, Los Angeles, and San Diego.

and how much, are tricky problems that are yet to be entirely resolved, despite legal and diplomatic battles. Even the authority of the United Nations has entered into the fray on behalf of Mexico, which receives water of ever-declining quality in ever-declining amounts.

As the twenty-first century moves forward, all those with a stake in the Colorado's health agree that the West's hardest-working river needs immediate assistance in the form of sweeping changes in the way it is used. Scientists are working to construct and implement strategies aimed at restoring the quality of the water both for agriculture and for riparian wildlife. Lawyers are also playing a role, renegotiating and rewriting water agreements drawn up early in the twentieth century that no longer address the needs of all users living within the river basin. Shifting population concentrations and changing water-use patterns demand compromises if all who benefit from the Colorado River hope to continue receiving its gift.

1
. . . .

A River in a Desert

The Colorado River collects and disperses more water throughout its small system of tributaries than any other river in the western United States. From its headwaters high in the Wind River Range of Wyoming and the western slope of the Rocky Mountains, the Colorado meanders 1,400 miles as it drains 244,000 square miles of watershed, an area embracing parts of seven southwestern states (Wyoming, Colorado, Utah, New Mexico, Nevada, Arizona, and California) and Mexico. Although the watershed is vast, the Colorado is not a particularly large river in terms of the water it carries, ranking sixth among the nation's rivers with an average annual volume of less than one-thirty-third that of the Mississippi.

The American Nile

This unusually narrow river, which has only a handful of tributaries, flows through the heart of America's largest desert. Searing heat, which evaporates much of the river's water, coupled with tributaries that add little to the Colorado's flow are two hallmarks of the Colorado as it struggles to reach the sea. Satellite photographs of the region through which the river flows reveal an extremely dry landscape. In these pictures, the river and its tributaries appear like nothing more than thin pencil lines amidst a parched, reddish-brown landscape void of greenery. Its journey through the American Southwest has earned it the name "the American Nile" because, like the Nile River in Africa, the Colorado flows through an enormous desert where more water is lost through evaporation than is added by tributaries and where the annual rainfall averages a meager five inches. Yet unlike the Nile, which floods every year, the Colorado generally stays within its very narrow bed,

The Salton Sea

South of the Mojave Desert lies the Salton basin, a large structural depression 235 feet below sea level, extending 150 miles northwest from the head of the Gulf of California. In 1905 floodwaters of the Colorado River caused a levee to break near Yuma; its waters rushed into the Salton basin, creating the Salton Sea, about 70 feet deep, 50 miles long, and 15 miles wide, with a total water area of some 300 square miles. Since the break threatened the agriculturally rich Imperial Valley and a major railroad route, the levee was finally repaired in 1907, but the Salton Sea remains.

The Salton basin is an 8,360-square-mile closed sub-sea level basin in the low desert of southern California and northern Mexico. The basin is actually part of the Colorado River delta. During the last thousand years, the Colorado River has meandered west and filled the basin at least three times, forming a freshwater lake called Lake Cahuilla. Each time, the river eventually returned to its more easterly channel, leaving the lake to evaporate.

The Salton Sea was formed in 1905 when massive flooding caused the Colorado River to overflow an irrigation canal and flow freely into the Salton basin for eighteen months. Since then, the sea's existence has been maintained primarily by agricultural return flows from the Imperial, Coachella, and Mexicali Valleys.

only rarely overflowing its banks—and then rarely by more than a half mile.

More than 90 percent of the Colorado River's basin lies within one of America's three largest deserts: the Great Basin, the Mojave, and the Sonoran, all three of which experience temperature extremes as high as 120 degrees Fahrenheit during summer and subfreezing temperatures during winter. The first desert the Colorado enters is the Great Basin Desert, which is also the largest of the three. Covering parts of Nevada, Utah, and Idaho, this 190,000-square-mile barren region averages 9 inches of rain annually. Just to the south lies the Mojave, which

The Salton Sea is beset by several serious problems. Because the sea has no outlet, water is lost only through evaporation, leaving dissolved salts behind and gradually raising salinity. The sea's salinity has now reached forty-four hundred parts per million, about 25 percent higher than ocean water. This elevated salinity might partially explain the decline in many fish species. The Salton Sea has unfortunately become known for its massive fish and bird die-offs. Fish kills due to deoxygenation have occurred in the sea since the fishery was established. Winter die-offs of tilapia, an African species introduced in 1964, are also common due to that fish's intolerance of low temperatures.

Dead tilapia fish line the shore of the Salton Sea during an annual die-off.

encompasses a portion of southern Nevada, extreme southwestern Utah, and some of eastern California. Its 25,000 square miles receive a meager annual 4 inches of rain. Last along the river's desolate route is the Sonoran Desert, covering parts of southeastern California, southern Arizona, and Mexico. Its 120,000 square miles receive the least rainfall of the three deserts, averaging just 2.25 inches annually. With so little rainfall along most of its course, the Colorado largely consists of waters it collects near its source. Most of the river's volume is accumulated along the first two hundred miles north and east of the deserts.

The Headwaters of the Colorado

The Colorado River begins its journey as winter snows accumulate between September and May along the fourteen-thousand-foot ridge of the western Rocky Mountains, which runs on a north-south axis through the state of Colorado. As the spring thaw begins, thousands of rivulets of pristine snowmelt trickle down the granite western slope. There, the snowmelt is joined by the melting remnants of five small glaciers left over from the last ice age, ten thousand years ago.

As rivulets converge along their downward, cascading journey, they form streams that in turn merge into small rivers gushing down to the base of the Rockies. Following a drop in elevation of about five thousand feet, several small rivers flow southwest across Colorado, working their way to Lake Granby, which lies at an elevation of 8,280 feet, between the cities of Boulder and Fort Collins. Because it is fed by this series of small rivers, Lake Granby is not the ultimate source of the Colorado River. Nonetheless, it is recognized by scientists—known as limnologists—who study bodies of fresh water as the primary collection basin for the river. Water from this eleven-square-mile lake spills out to the west, and it is here that the Colorado River officially begins its journey to the sea.

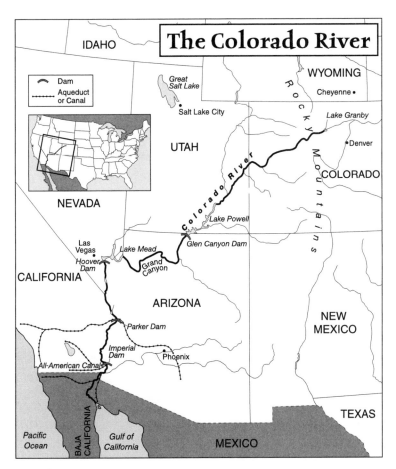

Tributaries

Most major rivers of the world collect water from hundreds, and in some cases thousands, of creeks, streams, and rivers feeding into them, but not the Colorado. This river has only five major tributaries that join it on its way to its mouth at the Sea of Cortés, also called the Gulf of California: the Gunnison River in Colorado, the Green River of Utah and Wyoming, the San Juan River of New Mexico, the Little Colorado in Arizona, and the Gila River originating in New Mexico and flowing west across Arizona.

The Gunnison River, the shortest of the major tributaries of the Colorado, flows 150 miles west from the Rockies to join the Colorado River at Grand Junction.

How much water the Gunnison contributes varies according to the season. The Gunnison is fed in the spring by snowmelt that swells the volume of the river to as many as forty-five thousand gallons a second to a late-summer trickle of only two thousand gallons a second. The Gunnison is known for its rapids, which are the result of the river's acute downward slope as it passes through several deep gorges.

The next tributary to join the southward flow of the river does so some twenty miles south of the town of Moab, Utah, where the Green River flows into the Colorado. The Green contains the water of the Yampa and the White Rivers, each of which drains the Wyoming basin. In this region, appearances are deceiving. Because it is covered with sage and grasses, many casual observers

The Green River winds through the steep walls of the Grand Canyon, eventually feeding into the Colorado River.

think the Wyoming basin is simply a low-elevation desert or prairie; yet this region is part of the Rocky Mountains, and average elevation is about 6,000 feet above sea level.

The amount of water drained from the Wyoming basin is also larger than appearances might lead one to expect. The Green River, which contributes a peak volume of about thirty-five thousand gallons per second when it joins the Colorado following a journey of 730 miles from its source, would contribute considerably more were it not for the dry high winds that constantly blow across the Wyoming basin. Thanks to these winds, much of the Green's water evaporates before reaching the Colorado River.

The third of the Colorado's tributaries is the San Juan River, which joins the main channel north of Glen Canyon Dam on the southern end of Lake Powell. Contributing roughly six thousand gallons per second, the San Juan originates in the San Juan Mountains in southwestern Colorado and drains 26,000 square miles of Colorado, New Mexico, and Arizona, or about 10 percent of the total Colorado River basin. As the river makes its 360-mile westerly trek toward Lake Powell, it loses about 80 percent of its water to man-made irrigation canals, which deliver its water to farmers in central New Mexico. In all, more than thirty such diversions remove water from the San Juan.

Draining a large part of northeastern Arizona and a portion of far western New Mexico, the Little Colorado River winds it way from forested headwaters in the White Mountains down through 350 miles of woodlands and grasslands and finally to the arid depths of the western Grand Canyon. The Little Colorado drains a 25,000-square-mile region and is famous for its striking bright blue color, which is the result of the leaching of minerals such as sulfur, copper, and magnesium from the rocks through which it flows. What begins as a fairly large volume in the White Mountains gradually evaporates over its course and delivers no more than an average of twelve thousand gallons per second to the Colorado.

The last major tributary is the Gila, which originates in the Mogollon Mountains of western New Mexico. The river flows east to west across southern Arizona. The Gila drains approximately 57,900 square miles before joining the Colorado River near Yuma, Arizona. The Gila winds its way, unimpeded, west 650 miles, and although it collects a significant volume of water from its watershed, much of the Gila's flow never reaches the Colorado River because it is diverted along its westerly route for use as drinking water and for irrigation.

The Colorado Delta

The river's last distinctive feature is the vast delta that forms near the end of its run to the Sea of Cortés. The delta is a broad, flat marshy area that forms as the river approaches sea level and departs from its narrowly defined course. Extending about forty miles from the river's mouth near Yuma south to the Sea of Cortés, the delta is slightly larger than one thousand square miles in area.

The delta is notable for the amount of silt underlying it. Geologists who have bored holes through the delta's sediment have measured its thickest deposits of silt to be ten thousand feet. Geologists explain that this delta is the result of eons of deposits containing billions of tons of silt carried down the river from high up in the Rocky Mountains. The Colorado River is one of America's siltiest, carrying an average load of 380,000 tons a day. Over several million years, the delta has slowly but steadily grown, displacing the ocean's water along the sea coast. Like all rivers, the Colorado carries the products of erosion—mud, silt, and sand—toward the sea. This debris becomes the building material of the river's delta. In this way, the Colorado River has poured over the face of its delta for millions of years, always only a few feet above sea level, building and extending it as the mass of the delta is gradually extended into the sea.

The Colorado River's delta is an expansive wetland habitat that provides a home for a variety of wildlife species, ranging from migratory birds to a variety of fish,

crustaceans, and small mammals. This thousand-square-mile area was at one time a morass of twisting river channels, marshes, and junglelike forest vegetation. Naturalist Aldo Leopold was enchanted by the river and its estuary during a 1922 visit to the region, and he later wrote,

> On the map the Delta was bisected by the river, but in fact the river was nowhere and everywhere, for he [the river] could not decide which of a hundred green lagoons offered the most pleasant and least speedy path to the Gulf. So he traveled them all. . . . He divided and rejoined, he twisted and turned, he meandered in awesome jungles.[1]

The gradual growth of the delta continued until well into the twentieth century, when construction of the Colorado's many dams and canals created vast reservoirs

The Gila River, the last major tributary, joins (from upper right) the Colorado River near Yuma, Arizona.

in which much of the silt settles. Hydrologic studies, made before construction of major dams, showed the Colorado was annually discharging enough silt to cover one square mile to a depth of fifty-three feet. That is equivalent to one cubic mile each century, cut from the great Rocky Mountains and from the canyons of the Colorado Plateau. With the construction of so many dams, however, the growth of the delta has effectively stopped.

The Great Buzz Saw

If the amount of eroded material that forms the Colorado's delta is worthy of note, a far more dramatic product of this erosion lies well upstream. The Grand Canyon is immense, a gaping rift as wide as eighteen miles and as deep as one mile, and scientists widely agree that the Colorado was the main force responsible for its creation. That creative process continues. As the Colorado washes down the canyon at a comparatively slow rate, friction with the walls and riverbed causes some bits of rock and sand to enter the river and turns the water a reddish hue. The friction of the moving water carrying sand and other forms of grit erode an estimated forty tons of sediment daily.

Scientists believe the powerful force of the Colorado River carved the jagged walls of the Grand Canyon.

The Colors of the Grand Canyon

Geologist Ann Zwinger provides both an artist's and a naturalist's view as she describes the Grand Canyon's walls while rafting down the Colorado in her book Downcanyon: A Naturalist Explores the Colorado River Through Grand Canyon:

"White streaks and big burnt orange patches of Hakatai Shale color the left slope above the rapid at mile 76.5. Some layers of the Colorado River contain brilliant purples and reds and startling patches of brilliant orange hornfels from the oxidation of iron-bearing minerals. When molten volcanic rock pushed into the shale, heat and pressure metamorphosed it to this vibrant color, which, where it outcrops, lights a canyon wall with hot coals. When polished by the rain it gleams like the elegant black and cinnabar red of Japanese lacquer ware."

However, this relatively benign erosion rate does not explain the sculpting of the Grand Canyon. Instead, scientists believe that such an enormous removal of sediment occurred periodically, when the river's flow was well above normal.

Evidence for this periodic sculpting occurred in December 1966, when a flash flood that acted like a buzz saw came down the canyon. Over just two days, continuous rainfall dumped fourteen inches of rain—as much rain as normally falls in the canyon all year long. As the water cascaded down the canyon walls and flooded hundreds of side canyons, the river began to rise. At the crest of the flash flood, the river surged forty feet above normal levels as it hammered walls that had not been touched by swirling water in many decades.

More than water raged downstream. Carried along with the water were tree stumps ripped out at their roots along with displaced boulders weighing as much as ten tons. Heavy debris such as this, swept along at high speeds by the rampaging river, whipped and tumbled down the river, slicing deep into the walls, and gouging out large chunks of sediment and more boulders. As the fury of the river continued for a few short days, the grinding action of the water and debris eroded more sediment from the canyon than would normally be removed over several years.

The Fauna of the Colorado

Natural forces such as the effects of erosion that created the Grand Canyon contributed, in part, to the types of animals that now inhabit the river basin. The dramatic change in elevation from the canyon's floor, where the river flows to the canyon's rim a mile or more above, means that average temperatures vary as much as twenty degrees. Precipitation may similarly vary. The result is a surprisingly diverse collection of animal life, although virtually every creature is directly dependent on the river for its survival.

Biologists working along the Colorado River estimate that as much as 80 percent of the river basin's vertebrate species either live in the river itself, live along its banks, or make use of the river as an important migratory stopover. Along the course of the river, seventy-five mammal species, fifty reptile and amphibian species, twenty-five fish species, and more than three hundred bird species can be found.

Of the twenty-five fish species in the Colorado River basin, ichthyologists have identified fourteen that are endemic. The most plentiful type of fish is the chub, a general term that encompasses such species as the round-tail chub, humpback chub, bonytail chub, Colorado squawfish, and the razorback sucker. These fish look like large trout or carp, grow to a maximum length of seven feet, and weigh one hundred pounds. The larger of the species are able to survive in fast waters, but the smaller ones prefer to inhabit tributaries and the calm waters of side canyons. This chub group, considered the big fish of the river, lives in harmony with smaller fish, such as trout, three species of which are present: browns, rainbows, and cutthroats. Smaller than chub, trout avoid the violence of the rapidly moving water in favor of small side streams and quiet wide spots along the river where they can find a plentiful supply of their favorite food, insects.

The trout and chub are well adapted to the Colorado. According to ichthyologist W. L. Minckley:

> Over 78 percent of the species of fishes now known from the Colorado Basin are peculiar to it. The unique features of the Colorado's native fish—extremely streamlined bodies, thick and leathery skins, small (if any) scales, and small eyes—reflected the severity of the pre-dam habitat.[2]

A bull elk wades along the bank of the Colorado River. Nearly all the animals living near the river depend upon it for survival.

The Colorado's fish serve as food for perhaps the most imposing animal of the Colorado River basin, the brown bear. Weighing as much as six hundred pounds, these bears prefer grasslands and lowland wooded areas close to rivers and streams. The bears are masterful catchers of fish. They wade into the water and, with lightning-quick flicks of their large paws, either impale a fish on their claws or flip it onto the riverbank, where the fish lies helpless until the bear retrieves it.

Of the many species with a high dependency on the Colorado River are grazing animals such as deer, elk, moose, and bighorn sheep.

During the cooler months of the year, these herbivores are able to obtain the moisture they need from the vegetation they eat. During the summer, however, these animals must drink directly from the river. Remarkably adaptable to the river environment, elk and moose are commonly seen swimming across the Colorado River in areas where the currents are slow.

The Flora of the Colorado

Fortunately for these large grazing animals, as well as many smaller ones, the river basin is home to all the plants they require to thrive. Botanists estimate the number of plant species throughout the Colorado River basin to be around twenty-five hundred. Which plants will thrive and where is determined by elevation. Closest to the river itself thrive species such as the pink-tinged tamarisk, the Fremont cottonwood that grows on the sandy beaches of the river, and colorful columbines and monkey flowers that dangle from layers of shale near the water.

At elevations two to three thousand feet above the river, increasing aridity of the soil allows only the hardiest of shrubs to gain a foothold. Here can be found an array of plants that are adapted to life in harsh, desertlike conditions. Flowering plants include some that observers consider the most beautiful, such as the cliff rose, fern bush, and blooming mountain mahogany. The cliff rose's gnarled branches bloom with creamy-white flowers early in the year, but the fern bush is a late bloomer, waiting until August to put forth its flowers. Mountain mahogany sprouts leathery leaves and a white plume flower. Some cacti grow in this region, and they flower in spring and then bear vividly colored fruit in late summer. Some of these species, such as Engelmann's prickly pear, beavertail cactus, grizzly bear cactus, and whipple cholla, bear sweet fruits that are traditionally used to make jams and syrups.

At slightly higher elevations up near the many plateaus above the river, a variety of trees, such as pinion pine, ponderosa pine, gambel oak, and Utah juniper, thrive. Compared to those closer to the river, most of the plants found here are relatively small, their growth stunted because of poor soil and limited water. Interspersed among the forest trees is a host of wildflowers that blossom between summer and fall, when warm temperatures arrive. Commonly seen are yellow sunflowers, golden western wallflowers, orange globe mallow, and rabbitbrush. Woodlands are awash in orange-red Indian paintbrush and purple hill lupine. Prickly pear cacti grow here as well. Also found here is the daggerlike yucca, which can be eaten and which yields fibers that were used by early river dwellers as thread.

The relative abundance of plants and animals, in addition to the reliable flow of the river, created a desirable environment for people as well. Some ten thousand years ago, the first inhabitants of the Colorado basin settled here and quickly gained an understanding of and appreciation for the river and its wildlife. As a source of water, food, and transportation, native peoples realized that in the river's environs they had found a place where they could thrive.

2

•••••••••

The People by the River

No element of nature played a more significant role in determining the pattern of life for the earliest inhabitants of the Colorado River basin than the river itself. From the Fremont and Shoshone tribes living along the northern Green River tributary to the Mojave and Anasazi tribes along the southernmost stretch of the river, all native peoples owed their existence to the river. Directly or indirectly, each tribe depended on the river as the source of its foods, medicines, transportation, and spiritual inspiration.

The identities of the tribes were inextricably tied to the river. Although each tribe was autonomous, each understood that the river created a common bond among them that gave them a collective identity unique to the Colorado River basin. The bond of the Colorado River was so powerful among the Indian tribes that they collectively called themselves *Pipa Aha Macav*, "the People by the River."

Some of the earliest Indian settlements archaeologists have unearthed are located along the southern stretches of the Colorado River. Radiocarbon dating indicates that their existence coincided with the retreat of the glaciers at the close of the last ice age, approximately 11,500 B.C., according to anthropology professor Scott A. Elias of the University of Colorado. These extremely old sites are

Sacred Rainbow Bridge

In San Juan County, Utah, immediately adjacent to Navajo Mountain and the Navajo reservation, stands Rainbow Bridge, which is only accessible by a two-hour, one-way boat ride from Wahweap Marina. Rainbow Bridge is the world's largest natural bridge, with a span of 275 feet and a graceful arch that reaches a height of 290 feet. The top is 42 feet thick and 33 feet wide. The bridge's predominant color is salmon pink with dark stains, called desert varnish, caused by iron oxide.

Rainbow Bridge is considered a sacred place by five Native American tribes: the Navajo, Hopi, San Juan Southern Paiute, Kaibab Paiute, and White Mesa Ute. For these tribes, both their ancient ancestors as well as current members, the natural arch is sacred because personified rainbows have always stood as guardians of the universe. These five tribes continue to practice religious ceremonies at the base of the rock arch although they are concerned that Rainbow Bridge— a religious and sacred place—needs to be protected and visited in a respectful manner.

This natural wonder was carved by streams as they flowed toward the Colorado River from Navajo Mountain's north flank. Until the formation of Lake Powell, this was one of the most remote and inaccessible regions in the contiguous United States. The first publicized sighting of Rainbow Bridge was made by the Douglass-Cummings party in 1909. Two parties had set out, one under government surveyor W.B. Douglass and the other under University of Utah dean Byron Cummings, to seek the great stone arch that Indians said lay near Navajo Mountain.

The base of Rainbow Bridge is composed of Kayenta sandstone, which consists of reddish brown to purplish consolidations of sand and mud deposited hundreds of millions of years ago. Above its base, the bridge is composed of Navajo sandstone. This formation was created as wave upon wave of sand dunes were deposited to depths of one thousand feet. Over the next 100 million years, both these formations were buried more than five thousand feet deep by still other strata.

rare, but there is a wealth of evidence of human habitation along the Colorado River in about 2000 B.C. Archaeologists have unearthed sites inhabited by tribes such as the Quechan, Pai, Havasupai, and the Hualapai. In fact, the name *Havasupai* means "People of the Blue Green Waters," and *Hualapai* means "People of the Tall Pines." But all of these tribes' histories and cultures were inextricably tied in one way or another to the mighty and sometimes unpredictable Colorado River.

Most tribes migrated between one of the many plateaus above the Colorado River and the banks of the river at the bottom of its canyons. The seasonal variations in temperatures and precipitation determined that most tribes passed the long hot summer months close to the river at the bottom of the canyons. There, they built huts,

First to Cultivate Corn

Corn was a critical staple to early American Indians and remains one of the few major indigenous crops widely eaten by modern Americans. Although some disagreement exists among agroanthropologists—anthropologists who study the foods of early peoples—most generally agree on the date but not necessarily on the first tribes.

The most widely accepted place and date for the earliest cultivation of corn is associated with the Fremont tribe that dominated much of the Green River drainage basin from perhaps as far back as 500 B.C. until about A.D. 1500. The Fremont developed a lifestyle that allowed them to successfully cultivate and store corn in a region where water and warm weather could rarely be counted on.

There is some contention that corn was first cultivated there as early as around 300 B.C. Traditional wisdom, however, puts the date for the first cultivation of corn somewhere around A.D. 500. Interestingly, corn was grown in the area right up to the arrival of Spaniards in Mexico. During the 1500s Fremont farmers planted corn. The Fremont stored seed corn in their small granaries, called wickiups, consisting of brush that they piled up and covered with river mud or animal hides. By living close to the water, native peoples could plant and easily irrigate their crops of corn, beans, squash, and other vegetables. In the winter they moved up onto the plateaus flanking the river. On the plateaus they found shelter in shallow caves or constructed huts made from wood sticks and covered with hides.

Early Agriculture Along the Colorado

For the many Native American tribes that lived within the basin of the Colorado, the river was the center of their agricultural activity. According to professor A. Dudley Gardner, writing about early tribes and their use of the plants they grew,

possibly waiting for the right environmental conditions; they planted corn only when conditions were right. Anthropologists theorize that the Fremont could predict the coming season by studying wildflowers, which told the prehistoric farmers when to plant.

Not all anthropologists, however, agree that the Fremont were the first. In 1999 R.G. Mason, writing for *Archaeology Southwest* magazine, proposed that the earliest evidence for maize cultivation in the greater Southwest would be found not with the Fremont in the northern regions but rather in the lowland floodplains of southern Arizona and New Mexico.

He further believes that the earliest dates are much earlier than those associated with the Fremont.

Mason believes that the cultivation of corn began in Mexico as far back as 3500 B.C. and that the technique eventually migrated north into the American Southwest. Samples of corn from regions in the southern parts of the Southwest date to 1700 B.C. Mason further contends, "One would expect the earliest maize-based villages to be found not on the Colorado Plateau, but in the Basin and Range Province to the south. I also reasoned that the Anasazi tradition, and thus the Pueblo peoples, might be the end result of such a process."

So intimate was the Native American's understanding of the plant resources in the area that they built their societies around harvesting plants. Native Americans lived not only on meat but also harvested plants that contained the full spectrum of vitamins. Moreover, some of the plants had medicinal values we are just beginning to understand.[3]

Where early tribes lived along the river determined the type of agriculture they practiced. In stretches where the river tended to rise over its banks and flood nearby lands, native peoples practiced dry farming. The canyons through which the Colorado runs for hundreds of miles were ideal for dry farming. This type of agriculture is not actually dry, as the name suggests, but rather refers to the planting of seeds in dry soil close to the river during periods of low water in the early spring. A month or two later, when the normal late-spring thaws arrived and headwater snows melted, the river would swell, and as the waters overflowed the riverbanks they provided the moisture the seeds needed to germinate.

Dry farming was a risky affair. If an unusually quick thaw sent too much water downriver, farmers might see all of their seeds washed away. On the other hand, a lower-than-expected snowfall high in the Rockies might prevent the river from rising high enough for water to reach the seeds and none would germinate. In order to allow for these two extreme conditions, tribesmen planted both close and far from the river. In this way, they could expect to harvest some crop even if it was not as bountiful as they would have liked.

By contrast, where the river flowed through relatively flat terrain, the native peoples practiced simple forms of irrigation. Archaeologists have discovered evidence of primitive check dams. These were stone walls, rarely more than three feet high, built across small streams. The water that pooled behind these dams would seep deep into the ground and provide the moisture needed by the corn and other crops planted by the Indians. Over time, as sediment built up, each check dam created a small field behind it that had rich soil ideal for growing crops. This type of irrigation was widespread. Evidence of ancient check dams has been found across the Colorado Plateau, extending as far as the southern reaches of modern-day Arizona.

In addition to check dams, evidence of primitive canals has been discovered. These canals, no more than one foot wide and eight inches deep, consisted of two parallel walls built of stones covered with dried clay to keep the water confined. Sometimes the canals were attached to check dams; when the dams were opened, water ran directly into the canal, which directed it to nearby fields. In their book *Hohokam Indians of the Tucson Basin*, professors Linda M. Gregonis and Karl J. Reinhard provide an overview of the agricultural practices of one tribe that relied on canals for irrigation:

Corn planted by dry farming techniques grows along the Colorado where the river floods its banks each year.

> The Indians built a complex system of canals to lead water from the river to their fields near the floodplain. Like other North American Indians, the Hohokam probably planted their crops in a series of small earth mounds. Corn, beans, squash, and cotton could all be planted in the same mound, so that each plant provided the others with nutrients and weed protection. Planted in March after the last winter frost, crops were ready to be harvested in July.

Villagers prepared much of their harvest for use during winter and spring.[4]

The Indians planted corn, beans, and squash for food and cotton to weave into cloth. They also relied on a number of wild plants native to the Colorado River's environs, such as mesquite, which produced edible beans, and many different plants whose roots could be eaten. One of the most utilitarian plants growing in the area was a type of cactus called yucca. This plant was the most useful because the long fibers found in its leaves could be used to make baskets, ropes, and sandals, and its roots could be ground to make a kind of soap. Archaeologists have also found evidence in fire pits of roasted chunks of the softer tissue of the yucca, an indication that parts of the plant were eaten.

Whichever form of agriculture the natives practiced, fertilizing crops was not necessary. According to Chuck Wullenjohn, a historian who studies the Quechan Indians who have lived on the Colorado River since 1540, "There was no need to fertilize, for there was a wealth of minerals and nutrients in the rich river silt."[5]

Sandal replicas made from yucca plants show various methods Indians used to secure the sandals to their feet. Indians depended upon many plants native to the Colorado River basin.

Hunting

All tribes living along the Colorado River supplemented their diets with protein from large grazing animals such as

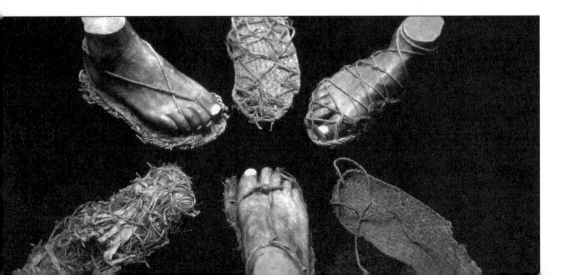

Archaeologists discovered spears used by the Anasazi to hunt large grazing animals. The Anasazi were a tribe native to the banks of the Colorado River in Utah.

deer, antelope, and buffalo that were plentiful within the river's basin. Occasionally, the Indians would also kill bears for their meat. The Indians valued all these large animals for their skins, which were cleaned, dried, and used for clothing and shelter. Hunting was likely even more significant for the earliest native inhabitants, who did not practice agriculture. According to Professor Elias,

> By about 8000 B.C. people of the Archaic [8000–1000 B.C.] culture were utilizing most of the Colorado Plateau. These hunter-gatherers did not settle down in villages, but probably followed the movements of game animals and gathered food plants through the seasons of the year. Archaic sites are common, though there have been few thorough archaeological studies of Archaic sites on the plateau.[6]

For many hunters, the river was significant. Archaeologists have evidence suggesting that when tribes sent out hunters to track down game, they set up camp sites located near the river. There, they could wait in ambush for their prey to come to the riverbank to drink. Excavations of campsites have uncovered the remains of hunting weapons and large caches of animal bones. Elias notes that the weapons these hunters used include "projectile points, sharp pointed heads of stone or other material, attached to a shaft to make a projectile that is thrown or shot as a weapon. These include spearheads, arrowheads, and darts."[7] Elias and other archaeologists believe that having the river as a source of water to lure game was critical to these early hunters. They note that because horses were not available until the Spanish introduced them in the fifteenth century A.D., hunting big game animals on wide-open plains regions would have been extremely difficult.

Besides these large game animals, the native peoples hunted a wide assortment of smaller animals, including rabbit, mice, and ground squirrels. Birds such as doves, quail, ducks, and geese were also caught. In more desertlike areas, tortoises, lizards, and snakes were part of the Indians' diet. Anthropologists surmise that small game animals were most likely trapped. Evidence suggests, for example, that during certain seasons, Indians conducted communal rabbit hunts. To prepare for these hunts, the Indians first dug long, deep ditches that gradually narrowed to function as a funnel. Next, they stretched a net across the narrow end of the ditch to trap the rabbits. Finally, when the net was in place, the Indians would begin beating the undergrowth, driving hundreds of rabbits from a large area into the wide end of the ditch. The rabbits, unable to jump out of the ditch, would run into the net, where they would become entangled and be easily captured.

Fishing

According to historian Wullenjohn, discussing tribal life of the Quechan Indians, "Men hunted rabbits, deer and birds throughout the year, but the Colorado River's abundant fish population made up the major source of animal protein in their diet."[8]

Depending on what sort of fish they were seeking, native fishermen could choose to fish from canoes, the riverbank, the shallows of the river itself, or platforms built in calm streams. The fish they sought and the conditions under which they were fishing also determined the fishermen's choice of equipment. For example, the fishing gig or trident was a spear with a three-pronged tip that was used by a fisherman wading in fast-moving but shallow water. When a large fish was spotted, the fisherman speared the fish, driving the prongs all the way through it. The fish could not swim free of the prongs because each had a barb at the tip that kept the prong from sliding out. Sometimes, the fish species being sought was large, with specimens weighing more than twenty or thirty pounds, and in these cases fishermen tied one end of a thin rope to the spear and the other end to their waists to prevent the fish from swimming away with the gig and pole.

A fisherman might also use a dip net, which was a saucer-shaped wicker basket attached to a pole by a long rope. A fisherman would lower the basket two or three feet under the water and wait for a fish to swim into or just above the basket. With a quick upward snatch of the pole, the attached basket would trap the fish. This technique required the fisherman to be above the water's surface, so Indians built small platforms on poles anchored in still waters several feet from shore.

The fishing weir was universally used among tribes along the Colorado River. Simple in its construction, it was a wicker or stick fence built across small tributaries or side creeks on a river. The wicker fence acted as a screen, preventing the fish from moving downstream. When a large number

Built across a narrow creek, a weir blocks fish from moving downstream.

were trapped at the weir, men and women with dip nets would wade into the water and scoop up the trapped fish. When they were done, they pulled up the wicker fence, allowing the rest of the fish in the river to resume their movement unimpeded.

River Transportation

The river's importance to the Indians was not restricted to its role in farming or fishing. The Colorado and its tributaries also functioned as vital transportation routes. Until the coming of the horse during the mid-sixteenth century, carrying anything but relatively light loads was impossible, so anyone with any amount of goods to transport traveled by water. The canoe was the preferred vessel for those traveling alone or in small groups. The Indians along the Colorado made two types of canoes: large, sturdy ones meant to carry many people and to be used for many years, and small, light-weight canoes meant for one to four people and intended to be used for only a summer.

The large, heavy canoes, commonly referred to as dugout canoes, were made by felling large trees, letting them sit for three months or so until they were dry, and then hollowing them out by building a small fire in the fallen tree trunk. The individual wishing to make a dugout canoe would smear resin on one side of the tree trunk and set fire to it. The charred wood was then scraped away and the process repeated until a sufficient hollow had been created. Exactly how many people these canoes might have held is uncertain because no specimens survive. However, archaeologists have discovered cave paintings showing as many as twenty figures in a single canoe.

Lightweight canoes were made by first constructing a tough but light wooden frame and then covering the frame with the most readily available material that could resist water. Along the northern stretches of the Colorado, where an abundance of trees grew, large pieces of thin bark were pleated and contoured to the frame. Sometimes they were sewn in sections and caulked with spruce gum to make the canoe watertight. Sticks were then added crosswise inside to give the canoe rigidity and strength. Techniques and materials used in building canoes varied from tribe to tribe and according to local conditions. Farther south, for example, where dry conditions prevented the growth of trees large enough to yield usable bark, skins from animals such as deer and antelope were sewn together, coated with tree sap to repel water, and stretched over the canoe frame.

Whatever the design or materials canoe builders used, the main danger was rapids, which would often smash these fragile watercraft. In such dangerous sections of the river, canoes would be pulled from the river and portaged past the danger zones. If the canoes were carrying cargo, rugged rafts, made by lashing several tree trunks together, were used to transport goods past dangerous spots in the river. When freight was well secured on the raft with leather thongs or rope, the rafts were pushed out into the middle of the river above the rapids and released to float without rowers over the rapids. Once the raft was past the boulders, swimmers would catch it, pull it to shore, and reload the cargo into their canoes.

The Spiritual Significance of the River

So complete was the natives' dependence on the Colorado for sustenance and transportation it is perhaps not surprising that the river had tremendous religious significance. Many of the natives' beliefs and rituals centered on the importance of the river, and most, if not all, tribes believed that life along the river was divinely ordained. According to researchers at Northern Arizona University, the tribes living along the southern stretches of the Colorado River "believed that their territory had been given to them by Tudjupa, their creator, who said, 'Here

Areas such as Horseshoe Canyon along the Colorado River held tremendous spiritual significance for natives.

is the land where you will live. Go to the places where you find water. Mark off your land and live by the water. Name these places.'"⁹ Many creation legends involved the Colorado River. One told among the Mojave Indians to explain the origin of the river is particularly colorful:

In First Times, there was chaos. And from the union of Earth and Sky was born the Great Spirit Matavilya. Before he could teach his people all they needed to know about the world, he was killed by his sister, Frog Woman. It was then that his little brother Mastamho took charge of the world and of the people. He drove a willow stick into the ground and drew out the waters that became the Colorado River, and with the river came fish and ducks. Mastamho made the mountains on both sides of the river using

One Indian Legend of the Creation

The many Indian tribes that once dwelled along the banks of the Colorado told many stories about the creation of the river. One of the more intriguing and picturesque is the Havasupai story that begins with a quarrel between the god of good, Tochopa, and the god of evil, Hokomata. As the legend has it, the creation of the Colorado River began when Hokomata threatened the land with a great destructive flood that would drown everyone, including Tochopa's daughter, Pu-keh-eh. In his book The Indians of the Painted Desert Region, *anthropologist George Wharton James recounts the Havasupai legend:*

"Working day and night, he [Tochopa] speedily prepared the trunk of a pinion tree by hollowing it out from one end. In this hollow tree he placed food and other necessaries, and also made a look-out window. Then he brought his daughter, and telling her she must go into this tree and there be sealed up, he took a sad farewell of her, closed up the end of the tree, and then sat down to await the destruction of the world. It was not long before the floods began to descend.

Not rain, but cataracts, rivers, deluges came, making more noise than a thousand Hack-a-tai-as (Colorado Rivers) and covering all the earth with water. The pinion log floated, and in safety lay Pu-keh-eh, while the water surged higher and higher and covered the tops of Hue-han-a-patch-a (the San Francisco), Hue-ga-wool-a (Williams Mountain), and all the other mountains of the world.

But the waters of heaven could not always be pouring down, and soon after they ceased, the flood upon the earth found a way to rush into the sea. And as it dashed down it cut through the rocks of the plateaus and made the deep Chi-a-mi-mi (canyon) of the Colorado River (Hack-a-tai-a). Soon all the water was gone.

Then Pu-keh-eh found her log no longer floating, and she peeped out of the window Tochopa had placed in her boat, and, though it was misty and almost dark, she could see in the dim distance the great mountains of the San Francisco range. And nearby was the canyon of the Little Colorado, and to the north was Hack-a-tai-a, and to the west was the canyon of the Havasu."

the mud of its banks. Mastamho gave the people the river and everything along the river. Whatever grew there was theirs, as he said, and they were the Aha Macav, the Mojaves, the people who live along the water.[10]

Even after someone died, the river continued to play a role in the Indians' spiritual life. For example, at death, the Mojave used cremation and the river to enter the spirit world. The property and belongings of the deceased were placed on a pyre along with the corpse. Mourners often contributed their own valuables as a showing of affection and then set fire to the pyre. Following the cremation, the ashes of the deceased were deposited in the river and the names of the dead were never again spoken.

The Colorado River was, at the very least, perceived as a place of spiritual significance where tribes could go to worship. The Paiute, for example, considered themselves spiritually connected to the river while they worshiped along its banks. Frequently, however, the river was itself believed to be a deity that should be thanked for its bounty. Giving thanks to the river was accomplished in a variety of ways, including a river-feeding ceremony during which tribal fishermen returned captured fish to the river as a way of demonstrating their appreciation for the food it provided them. And in religious ceremonies known as Keruk, tribal members would share some important object with the river god by placing the object in the water and watching the river carry it away.

The relationship between the Indians and the Colorado was one of respect. The Indians appreciated the river for the water that sustained their way of life. Because it provided them with everything they needed, they never sought to analyze the river or to change it. Such a reverence and respect for the river was not, however, part of the beliefs of foreigners, who mostly saw only the commercial potential of the river.

3

The Greening of the Desert

For 5 million years, the Colorado River and its network of tributaries flowed without interruption to the sea. The first people, arriving roughly 12,000 years ago, made their homes along the river without greatly changing either the river or the lands it drained. Even with the arrival of the Spanish during the sixteenth century, followed by Mexico's short supremacy nearly 300 years later, and then the American conquest during the mid-nineteenth century, the waterscape was scarcely altered.

The twentieth century, however, has seen change. As a network of railroads gradually spread across the Southwest, settlers began to move into the region, attracted by open spaces and cheap land. The economy of the western states surged, attracting to this arid landscape still more newcomers hoping to share in the new prosperity. As new residents poured into western and southwestern states, demands for water—and later for electricity—surged. When local supplies could no longer sustain the population, community leaders looked to the waters of the Colorado River as their savior.

The Arrival of the Spanish and Americans

The first Europeans to explore the Colorado River's basin largely used the river just as the Indians had—as a mode of travel. The Spaniards, who had conquered much of Mexico, wanted to be able to reach their settlements along the Pacific Coast. It was known that the overland route to the Pacific Coast involved crossing forbidding deserts. What the Spanish wanted to find was a water route from the Mexican mainland that did not involve a long voyage south around the tip of Baja California.

As part of the search for a shorter water route to the Pacific, in 1540 three vessels under the command of Hernando de Alarcón sailed up the Gulf of California until they entered the mouth of the Colorado River. From there, Alarcón sailed as far north as the confluence of the Gila River with the Colorado, at the present-day location of Yuma, Arizona. Alarcón named the river *Buena Guia*, the "River of the Good Guide," a tribute to the calm sailing it provided him.

It would be more than three hundred years later before anyone traveled upstream as far as Alarcón had. By the mid-nineteenth century, however, American pioneers and trappers were pushing westward across the Great Plains. They hoped to get rich from trapping beaver along the Colorado and its tributaries. They also envisioned using the river to transport timber from the forests of Colorado down to Arizona and California.

Standing in the way of the trappers and pioneers were the people who already inhabited the land. To provide some protection against the Mexicans and Indians who saw themselves as the rightful owners of the land, the U.S. Army sent troops into the area to explore and map the basin. What few seemed to see in this land was any potential as a place to live. One of the first accounts of the river, a journal written by Lieutenant Joseph C. Ives of the U.S. Army Corps of Engineers in 1858, made the point that

Wildlife Along the Colorado

Early explorers along the Colorado River depended on wildlife to sustain their exploration. In 1862 Sergeant George Hand of the U.S. Army wrote a diary about his detachment's experience scouting the lower Colorado near the Gila tributary. Judging from his entries, found in The Civil War in Apacheland, *Sergeant Hand makes it clear to his readers that food was the major preoccupation of the soldiers:*

"July 23, 1862—Left at 4 in the morning. Traveled slow. Killed one very large rattlesnake. Game is plenty—mourning doves, quail, cottontail and other rabbits very thick. Ferguson killed a very large buck yesterday. We have a shotgun but unfortunately no ammunition. Lots of the boys are at work with a seine catching fish. They are very poor biters and never try to get away when caught—no game at all. Very bony and soft. The natives call them hardtails. Another kind is humpbacks and flatheads.

July 24, 1862—Awoke at 5 in the morning. Had breakfast—broiled venison, coffee and bread. Some of the boys have already started on to hunt. While writing these lines I could have killed a dozen brace of quails and as many more doves if I had a shotgun. Took a cutoff, killed one deer—large buck. Packed him 1 and a half miles through brier and mesquite to the road, put it in one of the wagons and went on. Had several runs after rabbits.

July 25, 1862—We traveled on, every few steps quail, doves or rabbits, the former in large coveys, the latter by the dozens. How I wish for a shotgun. We arrived in camp at half past 6 A.M. I had a fine swim.

July 28, 1862—We were aroused by the breakfast call—coffee and bread again. Ten minutes past 2 A.M. we had everything ready and started through dust and bad road. Shortly after daylight I saw a large drove of bighorn sheep. Some of the boys shot at them. They were too far off."

the stretch of river that one day would be the site of Hoover Dam would never be of value to anyone:

It [the Grand Canyon] looks like the Gates of Hell. The region . . . is, of course, altogether valueless. Ours has been the first and will undoubtedly be the last, party of whites to visit the locality. It seems intended by nature that the Colorado River along the greater portion of its lonely and majestic way, shall be forever unvisited and undisturbed.[11]

Other Americans followed, including the best-known explorer of the river and the first to chart its entire course, John Wesley Powell. Powell was not the first to explore the river—Indians had been doing it for centuries—but he was the first to do so with the aim of advancing scientific knowledge of the river and its environs. On May 24, 1869, Powell and a crew of nine men began a heroic journey of exploration and discovery that would lead them down the Green River to the Colorado River and finally

John Powell's Biography

John Wesley Powell was born in 1834 in Mount Morris, New York, the son of a Methodist preacher. Powell developed an early interest in natural history and was determined to pursue his studies in science over the objections of his father, who wished he would become a minister. When Powell was eighteen, he began teaching in a one-room country school to earn money for college. The next seven years were spent teaching school, attending college, and exploring the Midwest.

In 1858 he joined the newly formed Illinois State Natural History Society, and as curator of conchology (the branch of natural history that studies mollusk shells), he made a fairly complete collection of the mollusks of

Explorer John Wesley Powell charted the entire course of the Colorado River.

to the ocean. Two years later, Powell conducted a second trip, following which he published his journals describing the geology and the wildlife along the river. His discoveries coincided with a period in America's history that witnessed an enormous and sudden influx of settlers all across the western United States, a time that came to be known as the westward movement.

During the remainder of the nineteenth century, a population boom occurred throughout the western states. This growth was fed by events such as the California gold rush, the building of the transcontinental railroad, and the influx of millions of European immigrants. The

Illinois. He began teaching at Hennepin, Illinois, in 1858, and in 1860 he became superintendent of its schools. On May 8, 1861, however, Powell enlisted to fight in the Civil War, and at the Battle of Shiloh a bullet struck his wrist and shattered into his arm. The wound was so severe that his arm had to be amputated below the elbow. Following the war, Powell accepted a professorship in geology at Illinois Wesleyan University in Bloomington.

By 1868 Powell was considering exploration of the Colorado River. He obtained some funds from private sources and from the Illinois State Natural History Society, and gained permission from the U.S. government to requisition military stores. In 1869 he made his one-thousand-mile historic exploration of the river, followed by a second trip in 1871.

Powell continued to study the Colorado River region for the remainder of his life. He became impressed with the problems of settling the arid western lands, and in 1878, encouraged by the U.S. secretary of the interior, he completed his report on the region, which was published as a congressional document. The book is considered one of the most important ever written about the western lands.

On June 30, 1894, Powell resigned as director of the U.S. Geological Survey. He had been in poor health for a number of years, and surgery was once more required on his arm. Powell's health declined steadily after his resignation, and he died at his summer home in Haven, Maine, in 1902. He was buried at Arlington Cemetery.

Powell and his exploration party prepare to embark on a one-thousand-mile journey down the Colorado River in 1869.

Native Americans, who had inhabited the region for thousands of years, struggled to maintain control of their ancestral lands but were eventually forced to yield to the newcomers.

A far more intractable problem, from the standpoint of the West's new residents, was the lack of adequate water supplies. By the beginning of the twentieth century, politicians, farmers, and land developers recognized that the Colorado River was the only major water source for the people, their livestock, and their crops.

The Imperial Valley

Typical of the Southwest's predicament was southern California. Booming metropolitan centers such as Los Angeles and San Diego needed water for homes and factories, and rural districts needed water for crops. The Imperial Valley, a desert region on the border of California and Arizona, had exceptionally fertile soil capable of high yields of just about every imaginable vegetable and fruit. The trick to the greening of the Imperial Valley, however, was a massive injection of water.

The initial solution was found in diverting Colorado River water south of the Mexican border back to southern

Powell's Journal

Perched in a chair firmly strapped to a small custom-made dory, John Wesley Powell pioneered the first documented river expedition of the Colorado River in 1869. After surviving the wild white-water rapids of Cataract Canyon, Powell continued along the river as it wound its way through the many carved and eroded canyons. The genius of Powell's trip was his ability to provide an excellent scientific description of the river as is evidenced by this entry in his published journal, The Exploration of the Colorado River and Its Canyons:

"August 22—We come to rapids again this morning and are occupied several hours in passing them, letting the boats down from rock to rock with lines for nearly half a mile, and then have to make a long portage. While the men are engaged in this I climb the wall on the northeast to a height of about 2,500 feet, where I can obtain a good view of a long stretch of canyon below. Its course is to the southwest. The walls seem to rise very abruptly for 2,500 or 3,000 feet, and then there is a gently sloping terrace on each side for two or three miles, when we again find cliffs, 1,500 or 2,000 feet high. From the brink of these the plateau stretches back to the north and south for a long distance. Away down the canyon on the right wall I can see a group of mountains, some of which appear to stand on the brink of the canyon. The effect of the terrace is to give the appearance of a narrow winding valley with high walls on either side and a deep, dark, meandering gorge down its middle. It is impossible from this point of view to determine whether or not we have granite at the bottom; but from geologic considerations, I conclude that we shall have marble walls below. After my return to the boats we run another mile and camp for the night. We have made but little over seven miles today, and a part of our flour has been soaked in the river again."

California. Mexico, however, charged a high price for this water, and a continuous flow was not guaranteed by the Mexican government: It could shut if off at any time. Still, by 1915 three hundred thousand acres of cropland depended on the diverted water. With so much valuable cropland relying on what was seen as an undependable water source, the need to reduce the cost and guarantee a continuous flow seemed clear. Calls for the construction of what was called an "all-American canal" that would divert Colorado River water directly to the Imperial Valley before it reached the Mexican border caught the attention of both state and federal lawmakers.

Led by Arthur Powell Davis, nephew of the famous explorer and geologist John Wesley Powell, promoters of the canal expanded the vision of unlimited water flowing to the Imperial Valley to include a great dam capable of controlling the floods that on very rare occasions wreaked havoc on small farms and towns in parts of southern California. Such a large dam would also be capable of providing hydroelectricity to western metropolitan centers, especially Los Angeles, where the population had grown 600 percent during the first two decades of the twentieth century. By 1920 the wheels were set in motion for the first great harnessing of the Colorado River, the construction of Boulder Dam.

Boulder Dam

In 1928 Congress appropriated $165 million to build Boulder Dam (now known as Hoover Dam). The project included the centerpiece of the project, Boulder Dam itself, as well as a second smaller dam, the Imperial Dam, and the All-American Canal. The stated objective of the project was threefold: to provide irrigation for croplands, to control the occasional flooding of the lower Colorado River, and to generate electricity.

The site chosen for the dam, the Black Canyon section of the Colorado River, sits about thirty-five miles southeast of Las Vegas, Nevada. Located on the Arizona-Nevada

state line, the site was principally selected for its narrow but deep gorge that cuts through hard granite walls. This gorge was narrow enough to be spanned with the concrete plug that would be the dam. In selecting the site, engineers also took into consideration the need for easy accessibility by some five thousand construction workers. Yet another consideration was the site's proximity to railroads and highways over which the millions of tons of construction materials would travel. The last critical requirement for the dam site was the presence of a large canyon behind the dam that, when flooded with water, would be able to store several years' worth of water for crop irrigation during times of drought.

Actual construction began in 1931 and was completed in 1935. Still considered one of the greatest engineering feats of the twentieth century, Boulder Dam was the

Workers construct the massive Boulder Dam, spanning the width of Black Canyon.

largest in the world when completed, and it still boasts an impressive statistical profile. Standing 727 feet above the churning waters of the Colorado River, the dam is 1,244 feet long at the top and 660 feet thick at its base. An estimated 6 million tons of concrete and steel went into its construction.

To protect the dam from flood waters spilling over the top and pouring into the interior caverns, where seventeen massive generators produced 1,344 megawatts of

The Concrete of Boulder Dam

The great uncertainty that swirled around the construction of Boulder Dam was the concrete. Never before had engineers dared a project the size of the dam that would be 99 percent concrete. Fears of the dam collapsing under its own weight, that the concrete might never harden, and that continuous pouring twenty-four hours a day, every day, could not be done. Engineers worked hard to solve these and other concrete-related problems.

The concrete was poured in blocks that were no more than five feet in depth. The blocks were approximately fifty feet by sixty feet on the sides. As each huge bucket filled with eight cubic yards of concrete was skillfully lowered

into the block, one of the half-dozen or so men waiting in the form would trip the safety latches on the bottom dump doors. The dam slowly rose in columns of five-foot blocks

A workman attaches a cable to an eight-cubic-yard steel bucket.

electricity per hour, engineers added two hundred-foot-deep spillways, one on each side of the canyon. Each spillway was large enough to float a battleship.

The Benefits of the Boulder Dam Project

The benefits of the dams and canal were immediately evident to the farmers of the Imperial Valley. As Colorado water poured down the eighty-one-mile All-American

because of the tremendous heat generated by the setting concrete. The Bureau of Reclamation had estimated that the temperature of the concrete would rise forty degrees while hardening and would take 125 years to cool. This problem was solved by laying one-inch-diameter pipe every five feet horizontally and vertically and running cold water through them to dissipate the heat.

No more than one five-foot pour was made in a column during a seventy-two-hour period, and no more than thirty-five feet of concrete was placed in any column within thirty days. Between each five-foot pour, a one-inch layer of grout, consisting of sand, cement, and water, was inserted to provide a bond between the hardened surface and the freshly mixed concrete. As the columns cooled and contracted,

spaces opened up between them. These were filled with a water-cement mixture of grout. An eight-foot vertical slot was left open in the center of the dam to provide access to the system of cooling pipes. When a fifty-foot vertical section of the dam had cooled, the slot was filled with concrete in ten successive stages of five feet each, thirty-six hours apart. Upon completion, the dam that was built in "pieces" was a cohesive, monolithic structure.

On the morning of June 6, 1933, the first eight-cubic-yard steel bucket, suspended from overhead cableways, dropped 800 feet into the canyon and disgorged its load of concrete. Pouring continued nonstop for almost two years. Day and night, bucket after bucket of concrete was dropped into one of several hundred individual columns for a total of 3.25 million cubic yards of concrete.

Canal at the rate of slightly more than one hundred thousand gallons a second, the acreage under irrigation immediately doubled, increasing to six hundred thousand acres. Within a decade that figure doubled again. More canals, such as the Coachella Canal, were subsequently built to supply Colorado River water to farms in California's Coachella Valley to the north of the Imperial Valley. Others were built to carry water to farms in parts of Arizona. By the beginning of the twenty-first century, an estimated twenty-five thousand individual farms were benefitting from the All-American Canal.

The secondary benefit to farmers in the Southwest was the elimination of flooding. Prior to the completion of Boulder Dam, an abnormally heavy rain and snowmelt in the Rocky Mountains caused the lower Colorado River to overflow its banks, sending billions of gallons of water over farmland. The flood of 1905, for example, destroyed homes and crops and heavily damaged highways, railroads, and irrigation works. In the process, water poured into a geologic depression between the Imperial and Coachella Valleys for eighteen months, forming the Salton Sea. This flooding formed California's largest lake, with an area of about 350 square miles. Since the completion of Boulder Dam, however, the Colorado River has never overflowed its banks, potentially saving farmers millions of dollars in crops that would otherwise be destroyed.

The third objective of the Boulder Dam project, the generation of hydroelectricity, was as significant to Los Angeles and other metropolitan centers in the Southwest as the water was to the farmers. High-tension electrical wires radiated out from Boulder Dam carrying millions of megawatts needed to serve the growing population and industries of southern California.

The industrial boom in southern California, which was initially driven by the construction of the Port of Los Angeles, a booming oil industry, and the burgeoning entertainment industry during the first few decades of the twentieth century, was given a second boost during World

War II. Beginning in 1942, the need for heavy war equipment such as ships and aircraft continued to fuel the growth of heavy industry. As the need for factory workers grew, a new influx of Americans, primarily from the South and Midwest, inundated southern California cities, especially Los Angeles. By 1950 the population of the city of Los Angeles had ballooned to 1.9 million and the metropolitan area had reached an astonishing 3.3 million people. Such an increase drove up the need for both electricity and water.

The All-American Canal winds through the arid desert, carrying water from the Colorado River to California.

Enter Los Angeles

Given the phenomenal growth of metropolitan Los Angeles, during the 1950s irrigating vegetable farms and orchards ceased to be a priority for Californians. Food for the teeming population of the Los Angeles basin, after all, could be grown almost anywhere and shipped in. Water and electricity, however, were both indispensable and dependent on a large river relatively close by. The electricity for homes, schools, hospitals, stores, recreational facilities, and factories could come from only one place, the Colorado River.

The community leaders of Los Angeles viewed the Colorado River as the savior of their city's growth and prosperity. Without it, they feared, the region's economy would flounder, the population would decline, and Los Angeles, as one of America's significant economic centers, would wither. The many entrepreneurs who had pinned their hopes and personal fortunes on the continued growth of the Los Angeles economy demanded more water and electricity. Although the Colorado River borders California along a short southern boundary shared with Arizona—less than 5 percent of the length of the entire river—Los Angeles alone needed 85 percent of the water and electricity supplied by Boulder Dam for its burgeoning needs.

A Proliferation of Dams

For political leaders in the region, the lesson of the Boulder Dam project was that the Colorado River could provide even more water and electricity if more dams were built. As demand for water and electricity for Los Angeles, San Diego, and the rest of southern California grew during the 1940s and 1950s, so too did the demand for more dams downstream from Boulder Dam. In response to this demand, major dams on the Green River and at Glen Canyon on the Colorado itself near the Arizona-Utah border were built. With the completion of these new hydroelectric dams, it appeared to state and federal agencies that everyone's needs for power and water were being met.

The additional drinking water and electricity were, however, only temporarily adequate. Although the electrical and water needs of most communities were being met, beginning during the early 1970s large numbers of Americans were moving to parts of the Southwest outside

The Colorado River Aqueduct

Although the All-American Canal is the most often discussed canal drawing water from the Colorado River, dozens of other canals also take water. One of the most interesting and unlikely routes of any canal is that of the Colorado River Aqueduct, which was completed in 1942 by the Metropolitan Water District in southern California. The canal takes water from the Colorado River at Lake Havasu, created by Parker Dam, and streaks across the desert and mountains in a generally southwest direction in concrete canals and tunnels.

In its statistics alone, it is an impressive engineering achievement. From the intake at Lake Havasu to the principal terminus at Lake Matthews in Riverside County, California, the main canal is 242 miles long. From Lake Matthews, another 430 miles of branches distribute water to Los Angeles County and parts of San Diego County. Its

capacity is 1 billion gallons of water per day, or about 1.1 million acre-feet annually.

At the intake near Parker Dam, two powerful pumping stations lift 4 million tons of water a day more than 600 feet during the first of several boosts to cross the mountains. The canal then proceeds by gravity flow for 70 miles to another lift of almost 150 feet. At Eagle Mountain and near Chiriaco Summit, two final pumping stations boost the water another 900 feet. The water has by now flowed 125 miles from the intake and has been lifted by pumps almost 1,500 feet, higher than the Empire State Building in New York.

The water then continues its extraordinary journey by flowing 115 more miles by gravity to Lake Matthews, near the city of Riverside. The total journey has taken the water more than 300 miles across the state of California.

of southern California. Growing metropolitan communities such as Phoenix, Las Vegas, Palm Springs, and Albuquerque began spreading out across the sunburned desert, turning it green with hundreds of developments with homes featuring swimming pools; expansive, thirsty lawns; and electricity-guzzling air conditioners. Developers also capitalized on the year-round sunny climate by constructing hundreds of out-of-doors recreation centers such as golf courses, theme parks, and water parks. For the first time, southern California had competition for the river's limited water supply.

The solution seemed to be the construction of still more dams. By the last decade of the twentieth century, twenty dams dotted the river and reservoirs stored water to be dispersed to thousands of thirsty communities and farms through a network of thousands of miles of aqueducts. So much water was diverted from the river to green the deserts of California, Arizona, Nevada, and New Mexico that none was left over to complete its flow to the sea across the border in Mexico. But from the American perspective, this was of little concern. As writer Philip L. Fradkin says in his book *A River No More: The Colorado*

In order to supply water and electricity to southern California, large hydroelectric dams were constructed on the Colorado River, like the Glen Canyon Dam.

River and the West, "Fresh water flowing to the sea was perceived as wasted, and had to be captured and harnessed to make the desert bloom."[12]

Recreational Use of the Colorado

Indeed, to American policymakers, the value of the large dams extended beyond water and electricity. The reservoirs created by the large dams proved a boon for recreational users who, prior to the dams, had been limited to boating down the rapids of the river and limited fishing. The large dams, primarily Boulder and Glen Canyon, changed the recreational offerings by creating Lakes Mead and Powell, which could be enjoyed by millions of visitors who annually came for boating, waterskiing, swimming, fishing, and camping.

Lake Mead is one of the largest man-made lakes in the world, covering 247 square miles when full. When full, it can hold 9 trillion gallons of water, which is the equivalent to two years of normal river flow down the Colorado. Its 550 miles of shoreline offer a variety of boating, skiing, swimming, fishing, and sightseeing opportunities. Lake Mead's surrounding desert offers many hiking trails and opportunities for wildlife photography. Lake Powell stretches from the Glen Canyon Dam in Arizona up the Colorado River through Utah, past the San Juan confluence to Hite, Utah, 186 miles north. This enormous flooded canyon has about 2,000 miles of shoreline and occupies 266 square miles.

The millions of tourists visiting the man-made lakes along the Colorado contribute millions of dollars to the economies of dozens of communities that did not exist before the building of the dams. The formation of the lakes has created enormous demand for hotels, restaurants, campgrounds, retail stores, and dozens of other small concessions that serve visitors' needs, such as lake guides and boat rentals. Just how much tourists contribute to the local economies is uncertain, but local civic leaders

Lake Powell, an enormous flooded canyon created by the Glen Canyon Dam, provides an aquatic playground for tourists.

view the surge in tourism as another benefit of the dams. According to Floyd Dominy, former head of the Bureau of Recreation,

> The Park Service estimated in 1963 when we closed the gates to create the lake [Powell] that perhaps 600,000 people a year might be using it by the year 2000. I predicted three million by the year 1990 and I was right. It attracts three million visitors a year. So the economic impact, just for tourism alone, would justify building Glen Canyon Dam.[13]

Environmentalists, biologists, and Indian tribes living within the river basin, however, do not share Dominy's jubilation over the economic benefits of the lakes nor the lakes' popularity as recreational centers. Unlike the vacationers who come to enjoy the lakes each year, many environmentalists and scientists are concerned with the health of the Colorado River. As the twenty-first century begins, there is increasing evidence that the West's hardest-working river is suffering as a result of too many demands being made on its finite water supply.

4
....

River of Controversy

The system of dams and canals constructed along the Colorado River, which were symbols of progress in the American West during much of the twentieth century, are now viewed by many as symbols of misguided planning, poor judgment, and out-and-out greed. The river, which once enjoyed a natural flow to the sea, is now blocked by dams at so many points and depleted of its water by so many canals that the natural flow no longer exists. As a consequence, wildlife, principally fish and migratory birds, have suffered as their movement up and down the river is disrupted and adverse changes in the composition and temperature of the water cause serious illness.

Dams Versus the Ecosystem

The huge dams along the Colorado are responsible for more adverse consequences to the Colorado River ecosystem than any other single factor. Their presence creates two distinct problems: Dams disrupt the natural flow of the river, and they prevent the natural migration of fish.

Philip L. Fradkin, in his book *A River No More*, makes the point that the environment of the Colorado

River has been so radically altered by dams that even so immense a feature as the Grand Canyon is really nothing more than an ultimate spillway for spinning hydroelectric generators. The release of water required to spin the generators is determined not by nature but rather by consumer demand for electricity. Fradkin laments this reality, noting

Dams built to sustain growing southwestern cities like Las Vegas, Nevada, have created many ecological problems for the Colorado River.

With all these changes [dams], it is hard to say the river and its immediate surroundings could be considered to be in their natural state any longer. But unless you whisper this repeatedly to yourself while floating down the river, it is difficult to realize that the Colorado within the Grand Canyon has become the ultimate ditch in the efficient transport of water from Lake Powell to Lake Mead for the generation of electricity.[14]

Flow management programs that control the amount of water spinning the dams' huge generators are geared toward meeting consumers' electric needs, causing unnatural surges of water that damage the river's ecosystems. When demand for electricity is high, enormous, sudden releases of cascading water crashing onto the riverbed create enough friction to physically scour the rocks of aquatic organisms and destroy whole fish populations. Other times, when the generators are idled, water may be withheld from the streambed for long or frequent periods, inhibiting riparian vegetation growth and stranding wildlife, especially insects and fish, crucial to the river's ecosystem. In addition, migrating birds find natural stopping places and nesting sites destroyed.

The unnatural release of water is only one of the dams' failings. Their monolithic presence functions like a concrete plug to migrating fish. Dam designers ordinarily attempt to build fish ladders, a series of concrete steps bathed in cascading water along the sides of dams, to provide passage in both directions for migrating fish. Such ladders, however, are not feasible on dams the size of Boulder and Glen Canyon. Without fish ladders, the migrating fish of the Colorado are permanently cut off from upriver migration to spawning grounds. Phil Hastings, curator of marine vertebrates at the Scripps Institution of Oceanography in La Jolla, California, says

> Dams lacking fish ladders force fish to survive in side canyons. Although some spawning does take place there, the survival rate is low because the fry [young fish] are forced out into the main river before they are strong enough to survive. That is why parents attempt to swim upriver to locate smaller, calmer, and better sheltered streams that protect their young while they grow.[15]

The prospects for fish swimming downstream are no better. If fish living in the large reservoirs swim close to the dam, as many do, they will be sucked through the

The enormous Glen Canyon Dam prohibits many species of fish from migrating to their natural spawning grounds.

dam in one of two ways: through an intake pipe feeding water to the hydroelectric generators or through one of the dam's floodgates that release water either over the spillway or through enormous pipes that channel the water through the dam and out into the river below. In either case, the chances for survival are poor. According to Hastings, fish sucked into the turbines "disintegrate from the spinning turbine blades"; he adds that that the survival rate of those forced through the floodgates is "not much better because of the turbulence in the pipes, sudden changes of temperature and pressure, and the impact hitting the river at high speeds when exhausted from the pipes."[16]

Declining Water Quality

The many dams and canals have also altered the quality of the river's water. One troublesome change to the

Colorado's water is a dramatic alteration in water temperature. Each large dam on the Colorado has converted a relatively narrow, shallow, and fast-moving section of the river into a very slow-moving lake with a large surface area and great depth. Unlike a free-flowing river, which maintains a fairly constant temperature, a deep lake separates into several layers of water with varying temperatures, a process known as temperature stratification.

A reservoir's top layer of water warms in the sun while the deeper water cools, creating a disparity of as much as thirty degrees Fahrenheit. Because the deep water is slow moving, the two layers tend to remain distinct. This stratification of temperatures accompanies a stratification of oxygen as well because the warmer water carries more dissolved oxygen than the cold water at the bottom. Because aquatic organisms must extract oxygen from

Jet skis speed through passages on Lake Powell.

water, this cold, deep water cannot sustain many fish. Problems arise when dam operators release billions of gallons of cold, oxygen-depleted water through large pipes at the bottom of the dam. This procedure artificially decreases the temperature and the oxygen levels in the water immediately downriver from the dam. Although many Colorado fish thrive in cool water, such sudden releases of water lacking sufficient oxygen have been known to cause large-scale fish kills.

In addition to altered water temperature, the dams contribute to rising salinity. Ten million tons of dissolved salts, such as potassium chloride, sodium chloride, and magnesium sulfate, are natural components of the river water. The majority come from salt-rich sediment that is picked up and carried along by the river. Prior to the dams, the natural flow of the river harmlessly flushed away the dissolved mineral salts. The problem that has arisen since the advent of the dams is that the concentration of salt is increasing due to evaporation of dam reservoirs. According to author Marc Reisner in his book *Cadillac Desert: The American West and Its Disappearing Water,* "Evaporation varies from year to year, but [it] averages close to two million acre-feet from all the reservoirs."[17] This rate of evaporation, from reservoirs alone, represents a startling loss of 11 percent when the flow is heavy to 15 percent when the flow is light. As the water evaporates, the dissolved salts are left behind, their concentration gradually rising.

Irrigation of land near the river itself further contributes to the salinity problem. Fields irrigated near the river receive billions of gallons of water annually, much of which seeps down into the soil, eventually finding its way back to the river. As the water seeps through the soil, it leaches more salt from the soil, so that water returns to the river saltier than when it left.

The river water averages about 750 parts per million (PPM) compared to a world average of all rivers of 140 PPM, making the Colorado the saltiest major river in the world. The farther south it goes, the saltier it becomes. By the time the river crosses into Mexico, it is carrying 1,000 PPM. By contrast, most of the drinking water in the United States contains less than 200 PPM salt.

Reckless Recreational Use

Meanwhile, the surge in recreational use of the Colorado River over the past few decades has come at a price to the river's environment. The millions of visitors who come primarily for recreation on the water in houseboats, water-ski boats, and river rafts are not only fostering various forms of pollution but also the manipulation of the flow of the river.

Of greatest concern are the thousands of gasoline-powered watercraft operating on the river year-round. Since the 1990s, most powerboats have been burning gasoline containing an additive called methyl tertiary butyl ether (MTBE), which helps prevent air pollution but is unfortunately a known carcinogen if ingested by humans. The problem with MTBE and the river occurs when gasoline containing MTBE is accidentally spilled into the water or when two-stroke engines that are used by the popular jet skis spew unburned fuel from their carburetors—typically about one-third of their fuel load. The MTBE eventually finds its way into the drinking water; cities throughout the Southwest have detected levels of MTBE that could only come from the Colorado River. Unfortunately, no filtration process exists that is capable of removing MTBE from the drinking water supply.

Pollution along certain portions of the lower Colorado River, near places like Laughlin, Bullhead City, Kingman, and Lake Havasu City, is particularly severe. This area has for decades been a mecca for weekend vacationers from southern California and parts of Arizona. Powerboating on the river is extremely popular, and gasoline from the boats pollutes this section of the river to the point that recreational fishing no longer takes place here. As casinos and resort hotels multiply, sewage treatment plants in the area are sometimes overwhelmed by the volume of waste, and untreated sewage that ends up in the river. According to writer Mike Davis, these communities are

Speedboat Racing on the Colorado

The major complaint leveled against the recreational use of the Colorado River stems from the thousands of various types of powerboats operating on the lakes and river that not only pollute the water with gasoline and MTBE but also disrupt the ecosystem with their propellers and jet-intake systems, which can kill and disrupt normal fish migrations. The worst examples of the disruptive nature of powerboats occur at the many annual speedboat races popular at Lake Havasu City on the lower Colorado River.

Lake Havasu City annually hosts dozens of speedboat races that attract tourists to the community but at the price of continuous disturbance to the river's ecosystem. Each year Lake Havasu City hosts regularly scheduled races and regattas such as the Trak World Championships, Campbell Boat Regatta, Shockwave Boat Regatta, Laveycraft Regatta, Tiger Boat Regatta, Carrera Boat Regatta, Commander Boat Regatta, Malibu Boat Regatta, Ultimate Boat Regatta, Advantage Boat Regatta, and still others.

Some of these events, such as the Trak World Championships, attract as many as 1,750 contestants racing jet skis in many different divisions depending upon the engine size of their watercraft. Contestants race around river buoys, churning the river while discharging gasoline into the river from their two-cycle engines, which have been banned on some waterways because of their notorious reputation for fuel spills.

Although not all of these events involve racing, all involve large numbers of powerboats that disturb the flora and fauna of the river. To emphasize the importance of powerboating to this area, one of the resorts on the river, London Bridge Resort, has this to say on its website: "However you like your excitement on the water, you will be sure to find it in Lake Havasu City: from soaring 300 ft. above the lake on a parasail to skimming across the water on a jet ski; from crashing across the waves in a speed boat to riding the wake on water skis."

a base camp for motorized toys—dune buggies, dirt bikes, speed boats, jet-skis, etc.—that each weekend make war on the fragile environment. Few western landscapes, for instance, are more degraded than the lower Colorado River, which is under relentless, three-pronged attack by the leisure classes of southern Nevada, Phoenix, and Southern California.[18]

Other recreational users of the Colorado also stress the river. For years, daily operations at the major dams were driven almost exclusively by the need for hydroelectric power. But by 1980, white-water rafting had become a highly profitable industry, especially in the Grand Canyon, and companies operating the rafts began applying pressure on dam operators to release unusually high volumes of water to accommodate the demand among thrill-seekers for a wild ride through the river's rapids.

These occasional large releases make for exciting rafting trips but damage the riparian environment. Although large releases occasionally occur naturally during the early spring following large snowmelts, environmentalists oppose accommodating the requests from rafting companies, which prefer that most large releases occur during the summer, at the height of the tourist season. Such large surges occurring at a time when the river would ordinarily run more slowly are harmful to organisms that are adapted to life in less-turbulent water.

Suffering Wildlife, Suffering Users

The wildlife is not suffering alone. Users of the Colorado River are now suffering as well. More and more groups that depend on the river now recognize that there is no longer enough water to satisfy everyone's needs. Before the greening of the desert that replaced the parched earth with millions of acres of cropland and hundreds of sprawling communities throughout the Southwest, the flow of the Colorado

White-water rafters traverse rapids on the Colorado River.

seemed sufficient to most people. Today, however, increasing numbers of people are facing the reality of a resource that has been exploited to its limits.

The limited supply of water on the Colorado River makes the river today the most disputed water in America. Many claimants have asserted their rights to the water, yet none is satisfied with the current allocation of this resource, which, in terms of the future development of the Colorado River basin, is worth its weight in gold. States are suing other states, and Mexico is suing the United States for access to more water. Largely lost in the battle to claim as much of the water as possible are the Native American tribes who were the first to occupy the river basin and who still live there yet cannot get enough water for their use.

Colorado River water is so valuable that virtually all the stream flow is used. The mighty Colorado, which rushes through the Grand Canyon in so spectacular a fashion, is a placid stream within a hundred miles of leaving the canyon and has virtually vanished in another hundred. During a cycle of dry years, all its water is either used or stored, and little if any water reaches the natural outlet into the Sea of Cortés. Only during a cycle of wet years, when all the reservoirs are filled, does any of the river reach the gulf. Such years are rare. During the 1970s and the 1980s, only four years saw water flowing all the way to the sea.

State Water Skirmishes

The popular notion at the beginning of the twentieth century that the Colorado River had enough water for all

Rafting the Colorado River

Seventy-year-old Colin Fletcher was the first person to raft the Colorado River from its headwaters on the Green River in the mountains of Wyoming fourteen hundred miles to the mouth of the river in the Sea of Cortés. He records his journey in his book River: One Man's Journey Down the Colorado, Source to Sea. *It is not difficult to imagine being onboard Fletcher's raft when he describes Cataract Canyon's rapid number 2:*

"Instant bedlam. Wells of surging white water, tainted brown. But everything straightforward. Just a careening rush. Small oar pressures to hold the raft at right angles to each wave, nothing more. The waves were big, though. As big as any we'd taken. But the bulging bow rode up and over them, one after another. At each wave water showered us with glistening off-white cascades that were cold, very cold; but the little raft held true. No twinge of danger, only exhilaration. Then we were clear, floating level, and I was scanning the right bank for a sheltered campsite, above rapid 3."

seven states within its basin has been entirely dismissed. As early as the late nineteenth century, a few farsighted realists such as John Wesley Powell saw problems looming. Powell predicted in 1893, while testifying before Congress, that the river's flow would not be able to meet demand, saying, "I tell you gentlemen you are piling up a heritage of conflict and litigation over the water rights for there is no sufficient water to supply the land."[19]

By 1920 it was becoming apparent that the Colorado River was quickly being used up. Southern California was home to most of the population of the western United States and was the largest and most productive agricultural region. The other six states that shared the river with California appealed to the U.S. Congress to determine water rights before California could get them all.

As an outgrowth of this appeal, delegates from California, Arizona, Nevada, New Mexico, Utah, Colorado, and Wyoming met before a Congressional committee in 1922 and negotiated the Colorado River Compact. The compact divided the seven states into two basins: the lower basin included Arizona, California, and Nevada, and the upper basin included the other four states. Based on the federal Bureau of Reclamation's estimated average annual flow of the Colorado of 17.5 million acre-feet (MAF), where 1 acre-foot is equivalent to 325,900 gallons, 8.5 MAF were allotted to the lower basin states, 7.5 MAF to the upper basin states, and 1.5 MAF to Mexico.

Quarrelling over the Colorado River Compact began even before work on it was completed. The seven states refused to ratify it. No one knew how to measure each state's usage, and southern California continued to take the lion's share allotted to the lower basin states without regard to complaints from Arizona and Nevada. Southern California's insatiable appetite for water prompted author Marc Reisner to note, "Southern California thrives, even survives, by moving water from where it is and presumably isn't needed, to where it isn't and presumably is needed."[20] Eventually, in

1928, Congress agreed to authorize the building of Boulder Dam and the All-American Canal if six of the seven states would ratify the compact and if California would limit its annual diversion of lower basin state water to 4.4 MAF. This left 2.8 MAF for Arizona and .3 MAF for Nevada.

All members agreed to the compact except Arizona. Its refusal to sign stemmed primarily from a clause specifying that California would be guaranteed its 4.4 MAF of the 7.5 MAF allotted to the lower basin states regardless of the total volume of the river. This clause meant that Arizona would not be guaranteed its 2.8 MAF in times of drought, when the total flow of the Colorado falls well below 17.5 MAF. In fact, most years the total flow is considerably below 17.5 MAF, usually closer to 14 MAF.

Explosive growth in southern California continued for the next fifty years, and as a result, the terms of the agreement continued to be violated. California exceeded its limits many years, and acrimonious debate and litigation between parties to the agreement have continued. Metropolitan areas such as Las Vegas, Phoenix, Tucson, and Denver have experienced booming growth in the meantime, causing them to demand more water and to threaten to shut down California's supply by closing off the canals that carry water to that state. The increasingly stiff competition for whatever small quantities of water remain in the Colorado River keeps the states in the Colorado River basin tied up in litigation and controversy.

Mexican Claims to Colorado Water

Among the users of the Colorado's water, Mexico sits at the end of the line. No location could be worse in regard to a river that regularly runs out of water. Ever since the epidemic of dam and canal construction began in America in the 1920s, Mexico has received only as much water from the Colorado as American states have allowed to flow there, regardless of treaty obligations. In times of heavy rainfall, Mexico has received its promised 1.5 MAF, but in times of drought, which account for sixteen

Citizens of Tijuana, Mexico protest the high salt content of the Colorado River water supply that reaches Mexico.

of the twenty years between 1982 and 2002, Mexico has received considerably less. Adding insult to injury, the quality of the water declines the farther it flows from the source. The water that crosses the Mexican border is so high in salt content that crops irrigated with it are noticeably reduced as compared with crops to the north. According to writers and workers for the Moving Waters project, a collaborative effort by humanities councils from seven western states to raise awareness about the Colorado,

> Upon construction of 20 dams and 80 diversions upstream, river flows to the delta have been reduced nearly 75 percent during the 20th century. Consequently there is less silt, fewer nutrients, higher salinity, and higher concentrations of pollutants. Today less than five percent of the historic ecosystem

remains. Still, the delta is the largest remaining wetland system in the American southwest.[21]

Fish have also suffered. Fishing remains a crucial source of income for Mexican communities near the river's mouth at the Sea of Cortés. Fish are still caught, but they are now smaller and fewer in number than when the Colorado flowed steadily into the sea, cleansing the waters and creating conditions ideal for spawning. A coalition of Mexican lawyers and environmental groups recently filed suit in the international court of the United Nations to force the United States to direct more water to Mexico. The hope is to receive enough water for the Colorado River delta, which is in danger of drying out and dying as a result. The coalition is seeking a dedicated flow of about .05 MAF a year to help the delta, plus an additional .4 MAF in rainy years—a volume that is still far below the 1.5 MAF supposedly guaranteed by treaty.

Native American Claims
The Mexicans are not the only ones whose claims for water have been pushed aside. Native American tribes, some of whose claims to the Colorado River date back thousands of years, have been accorded fewer rights to water than the Mexicans.

The difficulty that many American Indian tribes living in the Colorado Plateau experience in obtaining water for irrigation can be traced all the way back to the first negotiations of the Colorado River Compact in 1922. According to Joe Gelt, writer and editor for the Water Resources Research Center at the University of Arizona, regarding Indians and the negotiations for allocation of the Colorado River water,

> Along with working out their Colorado River plans and strategies the states also contended with various issues that delegates did not address and that later arose to prominence. Some, like environmental concerns, were not recognized as important at that time,

while others, like Indian water rights, were simply side-stepped by negotiators.[22]

Navajo tribal chairman Peter McDonald expressed a far less charitable view in 1979 when addressing a group of Colorado River water users:

The Federal Government has, over the past 70 years, aggressively subsidized and promoted the interests of virtually every water user in this audience. Only the Indians have failed to benefit. As I see it, the Indian's exclusion from participation in basin development has resulted from a silent conspiracy between the western states and Federal Government.[23]

Branchlike patterns in the soil from evaporated water at the Colorado River delta show the effects of water diversion.

Historian Philip L. Fradkin adds to the irony of the situation faced by one tribe, the Navajo, by pointing out, "The Navajos ostensibly had a greater claim on Colorado River water than any other tribe or possibly combination of tribes in the Southwest."[24]

Navajo tribal chairman Peter McDonald speaks out against the federal government's exclusion of Indians in water subsidization.

The water disputes that have become a way of life for all communities, states, and nations dependent upon the Colorado's water highlight the urgency of finding solutions to the fact that the Colorado can no longer satisfy everyone's water needs, no matter how hard it works. Scientists and politicians of the twenty-first century have begun working together to better utilize what water the Colorado River delivers because they cannot squeeze more from the river than nature will deliver.

5

....

Water, Deserts, and People

Water, deserts, and people are not a natural combination, and because the Colorado runs mostly through desert, competing claims on the Colorado make managing this vital resource increasingly complex. The scientists, citizen groups, and politicians who are the stewards of the Colorado River are now willing to consider a completely new set of standards to guide and manage water use. Some of the new ideas involve the use of new technologies for agriculture and irrigation, while others look to technology to return the Colorado to its halcyon times of good health and natural flow. Some conservationists even recommend the removal of the Glen Canyon Dam as a first major step in the right direction.

Other new ideas involve attitudes rather than technological solutions. One example of this sort of change is a rethinking of how water is used, as some leaders question the wisdom of growing crops in the desert when the same crops could be grown without irrigation in less arid regions. Demographers enter the fray by recommending that continued population growth in the arid Southwest, far from adequate and

Dire Water Predictions

Many years before the construction of Boulder Dam, proponents of the project who were eager to bring water into the Imperial Valley talked about the prosperity the water would bring and the unprecedented assortment of vegetables that would be grown there to feed the population of southern California. Years before the first drops of water appeared, real estate speculators drove up the price of land from five dollars an acre to as high as one thousand dollars. Because of the land frenzy and the limit on water, not everyone saw a rosy picture. One such man, who held a clearer view of the future of water than most, was John Wesley Powell. In his book The Grand Colorado, *T. H. Watkins quotes Powell, who had the following observations to make when asked to address a congres-sional committee investigating the irrigation of the Imperial Valley:*

"Not one acre of land should be granted to individuals for irrigation purposes. I want to say to you . . . the interest in these water rights will swiftly increase. . . . You are piling up a heritage of conflict in litigation over water rights, there is not sufficient water to supply these lands. There is no water to put on half the lands now owned by the Government. There is not water enough in all the arid region to irrigate the lands which the government has already disposed of. My prime interest is in such a system as will develop the greatest number of cottage homes for the people. I am more interested in the home and the cradle than I am in the bank counter."

reliable water supplies, should be discouraged in favor of metropolitan areas close to plentiful water.

Restoring the Colorado River to its pristine profile that existed before the construction of dams and canals is the most widely promoted objective among groups concerned with the future health of the river basin. Key to accomplishing this objective, short of the actual removal of the dams, is making two important adjustments that will improve the river's health: Reverse the disrupted and unnatural flow, and reverse the declining water quality.

Restoring the River's Natural Flow

Limnologists and biologists agree that when natural fluctuations in water flow are restored to a river, population densities of native aquatic organisms increase. Short of the removal of all dams on the Colorado, many river specialists believe that some of the natural flow can be returned if release of water from dams reflects the natural flow of the river rather than reflecting the demand for electricity. One of the natural phenomena of the river, which had not occurred since the construction of the major dams, was a torrential flood necessary for cleansing the river of debris and brackish water trapped in side canyons, which are detrimental to the river's wildlife.

Water pours from the Glen Canyon Dam in an attempt to manufacture the natural flow of the river.

Drain Lake Powell

In 1997 David Brower, president of the Sierra Club, an environmental organization with a long history of social and political activism, called for the draining of Lake Powell as the best solution to many of the ills that plague the Colorado River ecosystem downriver from the lake. In an article he wrote for Sierra Magazine *in 1997, Brower made the following observations supporting this fairly extreme position:*

"As surely as we made a mistake years ago [the construction of Glen Canyon Dam], we can reverse it now. We can drain Lake Powell and let the Colorado River run through the dam that created it, bringing Glen Canyon and the wonder of its side canyons back to life. We can let the river do what it needs to do downstream in the Grand Canyon itself. We don't need to tear the dam down, however much some people would like to see it go. Together the dam's two diversion tunnels can send 200,000 cubic feet of water per second downstream, twice as much as the Colorado's highest flows. The dam itself would be left as a tourist attraction, like the Pyramids, with passers-by wondering how humanity ever built it, and why.

Lake Mead's Hoover Dam can control the Colorado River without Lake Powell and can produce more power if Powell's water is stored behind it—saving massive amounts of money, water, and wild habitat. Economics and ecology are ready to team up on this one. Draining Lake Powell means more water for the Colorado River states and Mexico, especially Colorado and Utah. The hundreds of millions of dollars now being lost, growing to billions in the future, should be enough to give even Bill Gates [Microsoft founder and multibillionaire] pause.

The sooner we begin, the sooner lost paradises will begin to recover. The tapestries can re-emerge, along with the desert varnish, the exiled species of plants and animals, the pictographs and other mementos of people long gone. The canyon's music will be known again, and 'the sudden poetry of springs,' [writer] Wallace Stegner's beautiful phrase, will be revealed again below the sculptured walls of Navajo sandstone. The phrase, 'as long as the rivers shall run and the grasses grow,' will regain its meaning."

Normally, at least one such flood had occurred each spring prior to the dams.

To test this thesis, in 1996 the first of many planned major releases of water took place under the watchful eye of many interested groups, including Secretary of the Interior Bruce Babbitt. The stated objective in a massive flooding of the Grand Canyon, according to Secretary Babbitt, was "to restore the riparian areas and fish spawning areas that had been eaten away by the artificial river flows, fluctuating erratically from day to day and week to week only in response to power demands from cities as distant as Phoenix and Salt Lake City."[25]

On March 18, 1996, all floodgates of the Glen Canyon Dam were opened, allowing 337,000 gallons of water per second to cascade down the river. As Babbitt retold the experience, "I watched in wonder as the river surged, cascading a fountain of mist hundreds of feet in the air and flooding the entire length of the Canyon."[26] The release was allowed to run for seven days, during which time the water level in Lake Powell dropped 3.5 feet.

The results of the flooding were encouraging. The flood created numerous backwater channels, which are prime spawning areas and habitat for the humpback chub and other endangered fish species native to the Colorado River. There was also an immediate increase of floating organic matter, which is important to a healthy ecosystem because it provides nutrients for fish and other river fauna.

Biologists who were initially concerned with the well-being of fish and birds observed that fish swam to the bottom of the river during the flood and none appeared to have been harmed as a result of the flooding. Birds, including endangered species of eagles and falcons, flew to high ground to watch the event and then returned to the river when the water receded. The test was declared a success by all users of the river. Babbitt later remarked, "Restoration invites us to understand how the natural world functions as a whole. And the best unit to measure that whole, how it is more than the sum of its parts, is the river that runs through us."[27]

Improving Water Quality

Improving the water quality of the river has increasingly been a high priority for farmers, fishermen, and biologists. The two water-quality issues needing the most immediate correction are the salinity and water temperature concerns.

In 1973 the United States entered an agreement with Mexico to reduce the salinity of the Colorado River. According to Norris Hundley Jr., "The American negotiator of the agreement candidly acknowledged that unless the U.S. immediately took steps to control salinity within its borders another dispute with Mexico was inevitable."[28] In 1974 Congress passed the Colorado River Basin Salinity

A water research specialist monitors a desalination plant. Many efforts have been made to reduce the salinity of the Colorado River.

Control Act, which would not only benefit Mexican farmers but American farmers as well. The measure authorized upstream salt-control projects in Nevada, Utah, and Colorado, as well as desalination plants. The desalinization program reduced the salinity of the water going to American growers by roughly fifty-three parts per million, roughly 7 percent, of what it had been.

Unfortunately, the reduction comes at an enormous price. Current average costs to desalinate one acre-foot of water are running between seven and eleven hundred dollars. An acre-foot is equivalent to about 326,000 gallons, which will provide the needs of two families in a standard home for one year. There are many different types of desalinization plants, but the high costs, regardless of technology, are the result of costly construction of the plants and fuel needed to drive them. The most common type of desalinization plant uses the reverse osmosis process, in which a semipermeable membrane removes not only particles but also an extremely high percentage of dissolved particles, such as salt, molecule by molecule, from the water. Not only is the reduction relatively small and expensive to attain, but the process can create even more problems. For example, the world's largest reverse osmosis plant, located in Russia, is capable of desalinating about one hundred thousand cubic feet or about 750,000 gallons per day, but it is driven by a nuclear power plant.

Problems relating to water temperature and oxygen levels are also being addressed. Engineers have the capability of opening floodgates that release water down two spillways that do not funnel water into the intakes that feed the hydroelectric turbines. The floodgate water is warm oxygenated water drawn from the top of the reservoir. Engineers have agreed to mix water from the floodgates whenever large volumes are sent through the turbines. Biologists who have recorded water temperatures and oxygen levels immediately downriver are satisfied that the turbulent mixing that occurs provides water in which fish can survive.

New Irrigation Technologies

Even as researchers are trying to restore the Colorado's health, others are working to see that its water is used more efficiently. In particular, engineers are helping farmers refine

High-Tech Water Monitoring

High-tech solutions to locating and identifying changes in the chemistry of the Colorado River water have been initiated by both federal and state agencies. Pollution is a relatively minor concern in the river, yet because Colorado River water is used as drinking water for hundreds of communities both close to the river and as far away as southern California, constant monitoring will help maintain quality water.

Real-time monitoring platforms have been deployed in two Utah cities concerned with their water because they host water-sports competitions and wish to have the ability to continuously monitor for sudden changes in water chemistry anywhere within their water distribution network. The company that developed the monitoring platforms does not disclose the locations of their devices to ensure that no one tampers with them. Each platform has the ability to measure multiple parameters of water and transmit the data for remote retrieval. The testing equipment is then connected, directly or via unbroken cellular telephone data transfer, with built-in redundancy features. This data is monitored on an ongoing basis through the Internet, allowing local water officials to monitor for potential contamination of the distribution network on an around-the-clock basis.

Detection of changes in the water chemistry of the river that are of concern to water districts that provide drinking water to communities are also of interest to biologists and environmentalists. Not only will the monitors quickly signal changes, but they will also be able to identify any unusual chemicals in the water and then assist officials in detecting their source. Biologists working on the river will now, for the first time, be able to develop an accurate database of information that will provide critical data for many future generations concerned with the ecology of the river.

their methods to boost crop yields while reducing water demand. For example, farmers have long known that irrigation is most efficient on flat fields. Sloping or uneven land results in fields with excessively wet or dry spots where crops grow poorly. With the development and refinement of laser technology, farmers are now able to perfectly level their land and thereby increase crop production. Lasers are now mounted on bulldozers and other land-leveling machinery and are connected to hydraulic controls that automatically adjust the height of the blade or scraper. The result is a field that is free of irregularities where crop yields would be reduced.

Even with a perfectly level field, modern irrigation technologies can be applied to increase the amount of water reaching the roots of plants while decreasing water lost to evaporation. Growers of fruit and nut trees use

A new drip irrigation system provides a more efficient way to water these California grapevines.

drip irrigation, which delivers water directly to the root area of each tree by means of narrow plastic tubes.

Growers of row crops, such as beans, carrots, tomatoes, and other vegetables, can also use water more efficiently by placing plastic sheets over newly planted seeds and small plants, preventing the evaporation of water. As the seeds or young plants are watered, either by a drip system or even by flooding the rows, the water that would normally evaporate is captured under the plastic. At night, when temperatures drop, that water condenses and drips back into the soil.

Scientists are not just trying to help people use the Colorado's water more efficiently; they are also working to increase the river's supply of water. To do this, researchers are trying cloud-seeding to boost rainfall and thereby increase the amount of water entering the river. Cloud-seeding involves using airplanes to disperse chemicals, usually silver iodide, into clouds. The tiny chemical particles provide surfaces on which moisture can condense, forming raindrops. The federal government's Bureau of Reclamation has a pilot program for cloud-seeding in the San Juan Mountains of Colorado. Scientists working for the bureau are cautious in their outlook, however: "Cloud-seeding throughout the Upper Basin mountains would increase runoff by 1.3 million acre-feet a year. Although some find these claims encouraging, the overall feasibility of weather modification as a significant source of water must await the completion of current studies."[29]

Rethinking Agriculture in the Desert

However successful efforts to increase Colorado's flow might turn out to be, agronomists provide compelling evidence that growing crops in the desert is an inefficient and unnecessarily expensive venture to begin with. Many agronomists contend that water priorities should first go to cities, not farmland. To enforce this point, in extremely rare years when the Colorado's flow exceeds 17.5 million acre-feet,

Alfalfa plants, grown year-round in the Imperial Valley, require a substantial amount of water.

policymakers notify states in the Colorado basin that each will receive more water than the amount guaranteed in the Colorado River Compact of 1922. However, in 1998 the *Economist* published a story about these rare water surpluses, stating, "In particular, California will get no advance notice of surpluses until it stops wasting water in farming areas such as the Imperial Valley, and tries instead to reallocate that water to needy San Diego."[30]

Marc Reisner, author of *Cadillac Desert: The American West and Its Disappearing Water*, studied this topic extensively and supports the idea that irrigation is a poor use of water: "Western agriculture and livestock industries simply do not have a place in the West. The heavily subsidized, expensively irrigated farming of the West is no longer sustainable."[31] Reisner advocates increasing the importation of crops and meat from regions that receive adequate natural rainfall, such as the Northwest, Midwest, and East to lessen western reliance on locally grown foods that require irrigation to grow.

Some experts observe that it is the choice of crops that is the real problem in the American West. Researcher and writer Shannon Kelly takes aim at the cattle industry in particular as one of the most wasteful industries, noting

> Most of the crops produced, including heavily water-consumptive crops such as alfalfa, are grown to provide feed for cattle. Despite the enormous public cost of the region's elaborate water damming and diversion projects, the seven Colorado River basin states, including those portions of the states lying outside the basin and not receiving any Colorado River water, produced only 13% of the total value of the nation's livestock.[32]

With this thinking in mind, several large cities such as Phoenix and Tucson, which encompass areas of ranchland, began in the 1990s to discourage cattle ranching within city limits in favor of industries that could provide more jobs and use less water than ranches do. Many desert cities have successfully recruited high-tech companies to locate manufacturing plants on land that had once been devoted to raising cattle and alfalfa. Kelly pointed out to these cities that the computer industry, for example, utilizes water but can provide many more jobs per acre-foot of water used than ranching or farming can. Kelly estimates that each one thousand acre-feet of water used contributes to the creation of sixteen thousand manufacturing jobs in the computer chip industry—compared to only eight jobs growing alfalfa. During the 1990s Phoenix and Tucson, in particular, managed to attract billion-dollar manufacturing and fabrication plants from some of America's largest computer companies, such as Intel, Motorola, and IBM.

Economists have also highlighted the importance of moving fruit and vegetable production out of the regions dependent upon Colorado River water to areas where water is more readily and naturally available. Agronomists in California, the nation's most productive agricultural state, point out, for example, that the cost for vegetable and fruit production is higher in the Imperial and Coachella Valleys, both of which are irrigated by Colorado River water, than in the San Joaquin Valley, which is watered by the nearby San Joaquin River and its network of canals.

Changing Demographic Trends

The controversy over the Colorado River goes beyond the question of whether farms, factories, or people should be given top priority in allocating water supplies. Environmentalists are questioning whether the American West's population growth is sustainable. As populations increase, water demands increase as well, as more families demand parks, golf courses, shopping malls, and hundreds of other amenities that require water.

Demographic statistics gathered between 1900 and 2000 tell a story of unprecedented growth. Statisticians divided all counties presently watered by the Colorado River into five population categories, the largest two of which were counties with populations between 100,000 and 999,999 and more than 1 million. In 1900 only two counties qualified for the next-to-largest population category and none for the largest. By 2000, however, when the study was completed, twenty counties qualified for the next-to-largest population category and seven for the largest.

The region that receives water from the Colorado is now the fastest-growing area in America, a troublesome reality for groups concerned with dwindling water supplies. Some people question the reasonableness of continued urban sprawl across what is primarily a desert region entirely dependent on a river that is running out of water. To counter this trend, cities, community groups, and even some companies are for the first time attempting to discourage new growth and to encourage people to relocate elsewhere.

The decade of the 1990s saw the first attempts in southern California to limit the growth of communities as a strategy for avoiding water shortages. In the past, developers proceeded with construction before water supplies had been secured. As a result of water fears, a few communities initiated the strategy of stopping growth until developers secured contracts from the local water authority. This new approach has had the effect of slowing construction in some cases, stopping it entirely in a few, and reducing the number of units in others.

Corporations are also assisting in the slowdown of urban sprawl. Many companies located in the Southwest are now allowing employees to live and work in communities away from corporate headquarters in locations of lower population density and often wetter climates. Several high-tech companies in Phoenix, for example, are allowing employees to live in northern Arizona, where water is more plentiful, primarily in Flagstaff, and telecommute. This trend in the computer industry of living and working away from the corporate headquarters located in desert communities represents a small but growing effort aimed at reducing stress on the Colorado River.

Adjusting Water Distribution

Despite any efforts to reduce its reliance on imported water, California takes the biggest gulp of the Colorado River. There are two reasons for this, one based in law and one not. The legal reason stems from the Colorado River Compact, which allows California to annually take the greatest share of the water. Yet California regularly takes more than its allotment simply because it has the political and economic clout to do so. Many knowledgable writers have documented California's gluttony. Reisner, for one, states the case against California:

What began as an Olympian division of one river's waters emerged, after fifty years of brokering, tinkering, and fine-tuning according to the dictates of political reality, as an ultimate testament to the West's [California's] cardinal law: that water flows toward power and money, not necessarily downhill.[33]

As the twenty-first century opens, the federal courts are hearing lawsuits aimed at overturning the eighty-year-old Colorado River Compact. States with booming populations such as Nevada and Arizona are suing to take more water than specified in the compact. At the time when it was signed, only California was experiencing a population boom; now all are.

Meanwhile, policymakers are trying to address some of the inequities in the way the Colorado's water is meted

While California receives the largest amount of allocated water from the Colorado River, it wastes its resources on golf courses and other desert developments.

out. One of the more imaginative ideas for changing the distribution of water comes into play in the few years when the Colorado River actually provides a surplus, exceeding 17.5 MAF. The U.S. Department of the Interior has decided to allow the exchange of Colorado River water between lower basin states. This will immediately benefit Arizona, which has been storing its unused portion of the Colorado's water in underground aquifers. Under the proposed plan, it may now sell some of that water to other states, such as California. Water experts applaud the new policy because it emphasizes conservation. States that responsibly conserve water can sell it. Those who like the new policy call it "water banking."

Whatever politicians, scientists, and community leaders might do to reallocate water supplies or use existing supplies more efficiently, some observers question whether such efforts will be adequate to meet demand, which only promises to increase. According to a recent report sponsored by the Western Water Policy Review Advisory Commission, of the American states that will grow fastest between now and 2025, five are in the Colorado basin. The report goes on to say, "It may be fair to claim that the major period of settlement of the West did not occur in 1850: it is just now taking place, and huge amounts of water will be needed to sustain it."[34]

Epilogue
·············

A River No More

The title of Philip L. Fradkin's book *A River No More* is one assessment of the Colorado River that resonates with many who fear that the river's natural flow has already been overly constricted. It is difficult to argue with such an observation when one considers that dams and aqueducts prevent virtually any water from reaching the river's natural outflow at the Sea of Cortés—and more projects are scheduled that will further tighten the noose around a river that ceased to be wild decades ago. Others, however, while recognizing that the river is no longer wild, express confidence that changes in the management of the river combined with new technologies and more responsible water use can actually improve the present status of the river.

Such is the reality of a seemingly impossible equation of precious little water in an arid land experiencing the largest population increase of any region in America. The flow of the West's hardest-working river has shaped nearly all major western institutions dealing with water in general and the Colorado in particular. The dozens of laws governing the use of the river's water since the

Colorado River Compact was passed, and its many amendments and court rulings have made the Colorado what it is today. Each represents for its time what was perceived by its advocates as the best way of dealing with the river. The best way, of course, did not always mean the most efficient, the most environmentally sound, or the fairest.

The two groups most harmed by alterations to the Colorado's natural flow, the Indians and Mexicans, support environmentalists' efforts to bring back some of the river's wild natural flow. Several Indian tribes have expressed an interest in returning some of the wildness to the river for cultural reasons. Ancient burial sites located along the banks of the river that had once been under water for most of the year are now exposed because of the declining water volume caused by the construction of dams and canals. Thoughtless hikers sometimes pick up and carry away artifacts as souvenirs; worse still, professional collectors scour such sites looking for artifacts that will fetch high prices from wealthy individuals and even museums. To stop such pillaging of burial grounds, many Indian leaders support environmentalists' efforts to increase the river's natural flow more often, in the process keeping sacred sites inaccessible to outsiders.

Mexico would also like to see some dam and canal restrictions removed, allowing more flow. Mexican leaders know that such alterations would increase the likelihood of more water crossing into Mexico, improving crop yields while rejuvenating the delta area. The delta, which was a healthy, thriving habitat supporting a multitude of wildlife at the beginning of the twentieth century, could return to its former pristine state of health if the river were freed of some dams and canals.

Draining Lake Powell, initially viewed as an irrational and irresponsible solution, is now recognized as an act that would go a long way toward satisfying the needs of the Indians and the Mexicans. The only loss would be the hydroelectricity presently generated by the Glen Canyon

Unless limitations are placed on projects like the Hoover Dam, the finite amount of water in the Colorado will disappear.

Dam. As time moves forward, draining the lake and restoring its natural habitat increasingly appears to be a viable option.

As the competing demands on the Colorado eloquently demonstrate, water is a finite commodity. Experts say that during the next ten, one hundred, or even hundred thousand years there is scant likelihood that the river's basic supply of water will increase. The quality of life in the American West is inseparable from the river's fate. The significance of one of the world's hardest-working rivers is perhaps best expressed in the closing words of Marc Reisner's book *Cadillac Desert: The American West and Its Disappearing Water*, in which the author envisions "a region where people begin to recognize that water left in rivers can be worth a lot more—in revenues, in jobs—than water taken out of rivers."[35]

Notes

· · · · · · · ·

Chapter 1: A River in a Desert

1. Quoted in M. Cohen, "The Southwest's Great River," Center for Biological Diversity. www.biologicaldiversity.org.
2. W. L. Minckley, *Colorado River Ecology and Dam Management: Proceedings of a Symposium May 24–25, 1990, Santa Fe, New Mexico.* Washington, DC: National Academy, 1991, p. 137.

Chapter 2: The People by the River

3. A. Dudley Gardner, "The Green River, Living on the Land: Fremont Farmers and Chinese Railroad Workers." www.movingwaters.org.
4. Linda M. Gregonis and Karl J. Reinhard, *Hohokam Indians of the Tucson Basin.* Tucson: University of Arizona Press, 1988, p. 48.
5. Chuck Wullenjohn, "Quechan Indians Boast Long Colorado River History," National Park Service. http://crm.cr.nps.gov.
6. Scott A. Elias, *The Ice-Age History of Southwestern National Parks.* Washington, DC: Smithsonian Institution, 1977, p. 28.
7. Elias, *The Ice-Age History of Southwestern National Parks,* p. 30.
8. Wullenjohn, "Quechan Indians Boast Long Colorado River History."
9. Canyons, Cultures, and Environmental Change, "The Havasupai and the Hualapai." www.cpluhna.nau.edu.
10. Fort Mojave Indian Tribe, "Mojave National Preserve Mojave Indians—Beginnings," National Park Service. www.nps.gov.

Chapter 3: The Greening of the Desert

11. Joseph C. Ives, *Report upon the Colorado River of the West, Explored in 1857 and 1858.* Washington, DC: U.S. Army Corps of Topographical Engineers, GPO, 1861, p. 48.

12. Philip L. Fradkin, *A River No More: The Colorado River and the West*. New York: Knopf, 1981, p. 208.
13. Quoted in Moving Waters, "Glen Canyon Dam: The Consequences of Compromise." www.movingwaters.org.

Chapter 4: River of Controversy

14. Fradkin, *A River No More*, p. 117.
15. Phil Hastings, interview by author, July 2, 2002.
16. Hastings, interview.
17. Marc Reisner, *Cadillac Desert: The American West and Its Disappearing Water*. New York: Penguin Books, 1993, pp. 305–306.
18. Mike Davis, "A House of Cards," *Sierra Magazine,* November 21, 1995, p. 41.
19. Quoted in Moving Waters, "Dividing the Water: The Law of the River." www.movingwaters.org.
20. Reisner, *Cadillac Desert,* p. 243.
21. Moving Waters, "The Delta: One River, Two Nations." www.movingwaters.org.
22. Joe Gelt, "Sharing Colorado River Water: History, Public Policy and the Colorado River Compact," Water Resources Research Center. http://ag.arizona.edu.
23. Quoted in Fradkin, *A River No More,* p. 173.
24. Fradkin, *A River No More,* p. 173.

Chapter 5: Water, Deserts, and People

25. Bruce Babbitt, "Establishing Roots in Our Landscapes of Complexity," U.S. Geological Survey. http://mapping.usgs.gov.
26. Babbitt, "Establishing Roots in Our Landscapes of Complexity."
27. Quoted in Moving Waters, "The Colorado River—Background." www.movingwaters.org.
28. Quoted in Norris Hundley Jr., "The West Against Itself: The Colorado River—an Institutional History," Moving Waters. www.movingwaters.org.
29. Colorado River Board of California, *Annual Report, 1979.* Los Angeles: Metropolitan Water District, 1980, p. 12.

30. *Economist,* "Water in the West: Buying a Gulp of the Colorado," January 24, 1998, p. 18
31. Reisner, *Cadillac Desert,* p. 490.
32. Shannon Kelly, "Water Development, Extraction, and Diversion," Canyons, Cultures, and Environmental Change. www.cpluhna.nau.edu.
33. Reisner, *Cadillac Desert,* p. 307.
34. Quoted in *Economist,* "Water in the West," p. 20

Epilogue: A River No More
35. Reisner, *Cadillac Desert,* p. 412.

For Further Reading

Books

Frederick S. Dellenbaugh, *A Canyon Voyage: The Narrative of the Second Powell Expedition Down the Green-Colorado River from Wyoming, and the Explorations on Land in the Years 1871 and 1872.* New Haven CT: Yale University Press, 1962. Dellenbaugh tells his story of rafting down the Colorado River with John Wesley Powell. At eighteen, Dellenbaugh served as both artist and assistant. This book, written forty years after the event, provides an excellent and exciting account of the adventure and the nature of the river.

Scott A. Elias, *The Ice-Age History of Southwestern National Parks.* Washington, DC: Smithsonian Institution, 1977. Elias explores the mysteries of the Ice Age that include its possible causes, its impact on the ecosystems of the Southwest, and evidence for the Ice Age gathered from geology, paleontology, and archaeology. Elias also discusses in detail the interactions among ancient plants, animals, and environments.

Joseph C. Ives, *Report upon the Colorado River of the West, Explored in 1857 and 1858.* Washington, DC: U.S. Army Corps of Topographical Engineers, GPO, 1861. This document tells the story of Ives and a group of soldiers sent up the Colorado River in a fifty-four-foot iron-hulled steamboat that traveled up the rapids to the present site of Boulder Dam. Ives makes many interesting comments in his journal about the river and what he experienced on his journey.

E. Porter, *The Place No One Knew: Glen Canyon on the Colorado.* San Francisco: Sierra Club Books, 1963. This photographic essay is a poignant obituary of Glen Canyon. Intermixed with dramatic photographs of the canyon before it was flooded are short essays describing the environment and habitat for plants and animals about to disappear beneath billions of gallons of water.

T.H. Watkins, *The Grand Colorado: The Story of a River and Its Canyons*. Palo Alto, CA: American West, 1969. This is an excellent book covering the ancient beginnings of the Colorado River as well as its myths, conquest by dams, and its legacy for the future. The text is well peppered with beautiful color photographs of the river as well as old historical black and whites.

Works Consulted

Books

Colorado River Board of California, *Annual Report, 1979*. Los Angeles: Metropolitan Water District, 1980. This technical publication discusses in detail all issues regarding the use, distribution, sale, and management of Colorado River water.

Colin Fletcher, *River: One Man's Journey Down the Colorado, Source to Sea*. New York: Alfred A. Knopf, 1997. Fletcher traces the Colorado River in an entertaining travelogue as he rafts from its source on the Green River to the Sea of Cortés. As he journeys down the Colorado, he describes the river and its canyons while pondering the meaning of his life, his experiences in life, and his approaching demise. Although Fletcher is not the first to raft the river, he makes keen observations of the area's geology and wildlife.

Philip L. Fradkin, *A River No More: The Colorado River and the West*. New York: Knopf, 1981. Fradkin's book is a comprehensive history of the development of the Colorado River. Fradkin discusses in detail the politics of water in the West, who has made money off the dams and canals, who is most responsible for the declining quality of the water, and why it dries out just short of the Sea of Cortés.

Linda M. Gregonis and Karl J. Reinhard, *Hohokam Indians of the Tucson Basin*. Tucson: University of Arizona Press, 1988. This is an excellent book describing the lives of the Hohokam Indians based on archaeological and anthropological evidence. Both authors provide vivid descriptions of ancient sites that provide insights into their culture that covers topics such as their homes, agriculture, hunting, dress, crafts, and ceremonial rituals.

George Hand, *The Civil War in Apacheland*. Clovis, NM: High-Lonesome Books, 1996. A diary kept by a Union soldier serving in the American Southwest during the Civil War, this book contains accounts of travel and hunting in the region as well as accounts of occasional sightings of the area's native inhabitants.

George Wharton James, *The Indians of the Painted Desert Region*. Boston: Little, Brown, 1903. Although much of his book's content is outdated, James provides vivid depictions of the Havasupai and insights into their culture.

François Leydet, *Time and River Flowing: Grand Canyon*. New York: Sierra Club & Ballantine Books, 1964. Leydet wrote this book the year the Glen Canyon closed for construction of the dam. The book celebrates the timelessness and beauty of this region as well as the Grand Canyon in a poetic mix of words and pictures.

W.L. Minckley, *Colorado River Ecology and Dam Management: Proceedings of a Symposium May 24–25, 1990, Santa Fe, New Mexico*. Washington, DC: National Academy, 1991. This book contains many technical reports regarding the ecology of the Colorado River that were presented at a conference in Santa Fe in 1990.

John Wesley Powell, *The Exploration of the Colorado River and Its Canyons*. New York: Penguin Classics, 1997. Powell's discussion of his ninety-two-day trip down the Colorado River in 1869 is still considered the stuff of legends. The value of this journal rests with his serious scientific approach to recording, mapping, and surveying the route carefully. In addition, he described the flora, fauna, and geology of the area.

Marc Reisner, *Cadillac Desert: The American West and Its Disappearing Water*. New York: Penguin Books, 1993. This aptly titled book is a history of how the West and California in particular took water from the Colorado River to support a booming population and to create an economy richer than all but six nations. Reisner discusses the great water projects and provides valuable insights into the politics of water and desert ecology.

Ann Zwinger, *Downcanyon: A Naturalist Explores the Colorado River Through Grand Canyon*. Tucson: University of Arizona Press, 1995. Teamed with scientists and other volunteer naturalists, Zwinger was part of an ongoing study of change along the Colorado. In all seasons and all weathers, Zwinger rafted down the Colorado River. From the thrill of running the rapids to the wonder of the granite walls, she describes the excitement of riding along 277 miles of the river.

Periodicals

David Brower, "Let the River Run Through It," *Sierra Magazine*, March 13, 1997.

Mike Davis, "A House of Cards," *Sierra Magazine*, November 21, 1995.

Economist, "Water in the West: Buying a Gulp of the Colorado," January 24, 1998.

Beth Geiger, "What Made the Grand Canyon?" *Current Science*, December 15, 2000.

R. G. Mason, "The Spread of Maize to the Colorado Plateau," *Archaeology Southwest*, Vol. 13, 1999.

Internet Sources

Bruce Babbitt, "Establishing Roots in Our Landscapes of Complexity," U.S. Geological Survey. http://mapping.usgs.gov.

Canyons, Cultures, and Environmental Change, "The Havasupai and the Hualapai." www.cpluhna.nau.edu.

M. Cohen, "The Southwest's Great River." www.biological-diversity.org.

Colorado River Metropolitan Water District, "Fish Kills." www.crmwd.org.

Fort Mojave Indian Tribe, "Mojave National Preserve Mojave Indians—Beginnings," National Park Service. www.nps.gov.

A. Dudley Gardner, "The Green River, Living on the Land: Fremont Farmers and Chinese Railroad Workers." www.movingwaters.org.

Joe Gelt, "Sharing Colorado River Water: History, Public Policy, and the Colorado River Compact," Water Resources Research Center. http://ag.arizona.edu.

Norris Hundley Jr., "The West Against Itself: The Colorado River—An Institutional History," Moving Waters. www.movingwaters.org.

Shannon Kelly, "Water Development, Extraction, and Diversion," Canyons, Cultures, and Environmental Change. www.cpluhna. nau.edu.
Moving Waters, "The Colorado River—Background." www. movingwaters.org.
———, "The Delta: One River, Two Nations." www.moving waters.org.
———, "Dividing the Water: The Law of the River." www. movingwaters.org.
———, "Glen Canyon Dam: The Consequences of Compromise." www.movingwaters.org.
Chuck Wullenjohn, "Quechan Indians Boast Long Colorado River History," National Park Service. http://crm.cr.nps.gov.

Websites

Before the Cows (www.grazingactivist.org). This site is dedicated to providing eyewitness accounts of the West before the land was used as pasture for cattle.

Canyons, Cultures, and Environmental Change (www.cpluhna. nau.edu). This website is jointly maintained by several government agencies in conjunction with Northern Arizona University. Its focus is the region of the Colorado Plateau for providing information about the terrain and geology, the biota, Native American tribes, and changes taking place in the region.

Center for Biological Diversity (www.biologicaldiversity.org). The Center for Biological Diversity is working to secure a future for animals and plants that are nearing extinction. This site provides links to dozens of sites, and announcements discuss endangered species and their habitats.

Living Rivers (www.livingrivers.net). Living Rivers promotes large-scale river restoration. Its website provides information and links to other sites about reversing damage done by dams, diversions, and pollution. The website reports on investigations, litigation, and public demonstrations. The focus is to support alternative management strategies needed to bring rivers back to life.

London Bridge Resort (www.londonbridgeresort.com). This website is a commercial site for the London Bridge Resort.

Moving Waters: The Colorado River and the West (www.moving waters.org). The aim of the website is to generate regional awareness of the importance of the river. The website project addresses three themes: the geological, historical, environmental, and technological forces that shape the Colorado River basin, the laws that apply to the river, and the literary arts and folklore associated with the river.

National Park Service (www.nps.gov). This site provides links to all national parks throughout the United States. In addition to many useful pieces of information, extensive profiles are included about native tribes that occupy or once occupied park territory.

University of Colorado at Denver (carbon.cudenver.edu). This is the official website of the University of Colorado. In addition to student information and general university information, it includes research carried out along the Colorado River.

U.S. Geological Survey (www.usgs.gov). This website is a compendium of data pertaining to natural parks and hundreds of geographical regions of critical importance to America. This site provides geological, environmental, and biological data for thousands of critical regions throughout the United States.

Water Resources Research Center (ag.arizona.edu/AZWATER/main.html). This website is operated by the University of Arizona, and its focus is to communicate water-related research needs from research users to researchers and to report research findings to the public.

Index

· · · · · · · · ·

Picture Credits

• • • • • • • • • • • • • • • • • • • •

About the Author

James Barter is the author of more than a dozen nonfiction books for middle school students. He received his undergraduate degree in history and classics at the University of California Berkeley followed by graduate studies in ancient history and archaeology at the University of Pennsylvania. Mr. Barter has taught history as well as Latin and Greek.

A Fulbright scholar at the American Academy in Rome, Mr. Barter worked on archaeological sites in and around the city as well as on sites in the Naples area. Mr. Barter also has worked and traveled extensively in Greece. He currently lives in Rancho Santa Fe, California, with his seventeen-year-old daughter, Kalista.